IN & OUT OF SERVICE

written by
Ian Read & Guy Marriott

edited & designed by
Ray Stenning

picture restoration by
Ray Stenning

printed by
Lavenham Press

published by
Best Impressions 15 Starfield Road, London W12 9SN

with proceeds to the London Bus Museum

a superb **Classic Bus** production
for the London Bus Museum

ISBN 978 0 9565740 7 7

FOREWORD BY

**Peter, Lord Hendy of Richmond Hill,
of Imber in the County of Wiltshire**

Ian Read, one of the co-authors of this book, sadly died in 2022 after the text had been completed for this book.

Ian was knowledgeable on the history of the London bus, a good writer, a calm and unflappable driver of many of the historic vehicles described in this book and tackled every task with an air of quiet competence. He will be missed by many.

This book is dedicated to Ian's memory.

Of all the many things described as 'iconic', the London bus is one of the most deserving. No picture, film or even thought of London is without a London bus, or several. And that's been true for way over a hundred years. Transport for London, London Transport, and the London General Omnibus Company all know or knew it, and they also knew that the place in history of the London bus would be enriched by keeping for posterity historic vehicles.

That's the origin of the London Transport Museum, and now excellently complemented by the London Bus Museum at Brooklands – the latter wholly the work of volunteer enthusiasts – beautifully bringing to life generations of London's buses, both in static and operational form.

My own career, from conducting and driving Continental Pioneer's route 235 up Richmond Hill, and then London Transport's Routemasters in service, right up to my time as Commissioner of Transport for London from 2006 to 2015 (and now also as President of the London Bus Museum) covers many of the vehicle types in this book, and I still enjoy driving some of these buses now.

This great book looks at many of the most notable of these buses and coaches, their life in service and their more recent histories. It presents the work of many in ensuring the survival and restoration of a long line of buses which have served London and Londoners, and explains the place of each of them in history. Many of them can be travelled on in service, and most of the rest seen on display. I hope this book will encourage you to visit them on display, and ride on them when possible.

Both the Museums are charities, and this book, edited by Ray Stenning at Best Impressions, is published for the London Bus Museum and proceeds from this book will generously go to maintaining and upgrading the Museum and its vehicles.

I hope you buy it, enjoy the contents, visit the museums, and buy another for a friend!

FOREWORD BY

Leon Daniels OBE
Chair London Bus Preservation Trust

London bus preservation has really come of age. From the faltering steps of the earliest preservationists in the 1950s a large collection of vehicles from across the decades is not only secured but many of them are on display to the public, at our museums, and able to be seen and travelled on at various events across the capital.

We recognise Prince Marshall as the founder of the private preservation movement. Although he died in 1981, a few of the early pioneers are still with us and have seen their original projects turned into living, working vehicles. In turn this has inspired others to search, rescue, fund and restore more vehicles from every generation of London's bus history.

In this book we chronicle the London Bus Museum fleet plus other notable vehicles in preservation. Never could the original pioneers have ever imagined so many beautifully restored vehicles and so many of them on public display.

As in the London Bus Museum itself, this book seeks to tell a story to the world of the development of the London bus from its earliest horse-bus days to the latest zero emission vehicles. The red bus has always been an icon in the capital but in London bus history there have been many colours, shapes and sizes for different markets and operating conditions. We bring them all together here, showing not only the collection as it is today but also the buses as they were when in service. Where possible this is the actual vehicle; otherwise one very much like it in its typical surroundings of bygone London.

The genesis of this book was the donation of photographs of our collection of buses in service by the legendary Alan B Cross, who started photographing London buses in the 1940s. Thanks to him we can see many of our vehicles 'at home'.

The London Bus Museum is very grateful to Ray Stenning, who has designed and created this beautiful book for us as his contribution to all our work.

Finally, grateful thanks to our authors and contributors who provided photographs and comments on the text. Sadly soon after the authors delivered their final draft, Ian Read died suddenly. He will be greatly missed at both the London Bus Museum and the London Transport Museum – he was a frequent volunteer at both. This book is dedicated to his memory. Guy Marriott has finished the work they started together.

The London Bus Museum is run entirely by volunteers. By purchasing this book you are helping in our efforts. If it inspires you to contribute some more, either as a volunteer or as a benefactor, we would be delighted to hear from you.

FOREWORD BY

Sam Mullins OBE

Director London Transport Museum

My earliest memories of travelling by bus were aged seven or eight around 1960; I went to my first school on the bus, taking the 55 Wilts & Dorset service from the end of my road in East Harnham, Salisbury, to the Queensbury Stores stop on the Netherhampton Road, and then walking around the corner to the surviving World War Two Nissen huts in which West Harnham Infants' School was accommodated.

Later I recollect Saturdays waiting for the red 55 bus to take me home from the Market Place stands in Salisbury; I sought out the moquette covered bench seat on the left just inside the platform, buying a printed red ticket which came clattering from the conductor's Setright machine, looking down the cream and rexine lower saloon across the ranks of seats and handrails to the gearbox hump and the driver's back, waiting for the bell to be rung and the driver to turn the red indicator and pull out from the stand.

These early experiences have stayed with me. I now know that those buses were Bristol Lodekkas, and as a transport museum curator I have acquired a Wilts & Dorset bus blind, tickets and bus stop flags, and know the history of Salisbury's red buses since 1914.

But this is more than mere nostalgia; the experience of being moved by bus or train stays with us, becomes part of who we are, a touchstone for our younger selves, a window onto our past. This is the emotional motivating power for the remarkable preservation movement of our generation to continue the operation of vintage vehicles. This kinetic experience recreates and reinforces those memories, gives us a sense of comfort and self-awareness, a fixed point in a fast-changing world.

It is humbling to trace the heroic preservation of the cavalcade of buses in this book. These iconic survivors are related as both public transport workhorses and as the objects of painstaking recovery and restoration. I am sure this beautifully produced book will garner support for the missions of both the London Bus Museum and the London Transport Museum to offer the unique experience of riding on these vehicles, feeling the vibrations, sitting on the fabric, hearing the engine notes and the gears mesh, the clicking whirl of the ticket machine, and seeing the driver's mysterious skills at work.

It is both a pleasure and an honour to recommend *In and Out of Service* to you.

introduction

There are many iconic images of London known the world over – Tower Bridge, Big Ben, the black London taxi, the red telephone box – and, of course, the red London double-decker bus. Although today's London buses are mostly hybrid or electric, with front entrance and centre exit, and engine at the rear, the image usually seen on postcards is that of the traditional rear-entrance bus with a driver in the cab up front alongside a bonneted engine and the open rear platform to jump on and off under the supervision of the conductor.

But London buses have come in many different shapes, sizes, layouts and colours, as you will see as you turn the pages of this book that pays tribute to over sixty London buses that have been preserved, and represent a heritage that future generations can learn from and enjoy.

why preserve a London bus?

I t occasions no surprise when someone admits to being a train or railway enthusiast. For those over a certain age, the magic of a steam locomotive in everyday use with its appeal to so many of our senses is never forgotten, and with the large number of preserved steam railways in the country, and regular steam trains on the national rail network, all ages can enjoy the heritage railway movement.

This is well accepted, not just for the nostalgia it generates, but also for its contribution to the tourist economy in many parts of the country. Classic cars, too, are regularly to be seen on the road and, whether in motion or on display, give rise to a certain nostalgia – the sense of times past.

But an enthusiasm for a classic bus or coach, or another type of commercial vehicle, is perhaps regarded as a little out of the ordinary. And yet the classic bus and commercial vehicle preservation movement has thousands of supporters throughout the country.

It was in the early 1960s that London bus enthusiasts began to get themselves organised. The London Omnibus Traction Society (LOTS) was formed and is still going strong today; the London Bus Preservation Group (LBPG) dates from a little after the foundation of LOTS. More on the early history of the LBPG and how it developed appears later in this Introduction. The LBPG became in due course the London Bus Preservation Trust (LBPT), the charity which is the owner and operator of today's London Bus Museum at Brooklands. LOTS came to specialise in current and former London bus operations, whereas the LBPG concentrated on the vehicles.

It was LOTS members who first took ex-London RT1431 into preservation, shown in the accompanying picture on this page.

The story in this book is that of London's buses, and the development of the bus in London is not always the story of how buses developed beyond London and the Home Counties. Sometimes developments in London anticipated how the rest of the country would go, but often London was behind the times in developments elsewhere, because the size of London's bus operations, and the real or imagined differences in 'what London needed' allowed the London operators (mostly a monopoly or quasi-monopoly) to go their own way.

Most of the buses illustrated in this book as out of service (almost all in a working, roadworthy condition) may be seen, whether at the London Bus Museum, or elsewhere on display, or on the road. We strive for historical accuracy in restoration, consistent with the need, as running vehicles, to be able to operate safely on today's roads. And for the oldest buses in this book, the story of how they have survived is often as interesting as the vehicles themselves.

Below, former London RT1431 was being collected from its subsequent operator A1 Service of Ardrossan in Scotland in 1966. Left to right were Colin Stannard, John Bell, Mick Palmer and John Warner. With several owners over the years, the bus was acquired by Ensignbus in 2004 and features in this book.

the first London bus

The first operation in London of what we now regard as a bus was by George Shillibeer in 1829 on a route from Paddington to the Bank of England in the City. This was with a horse-drawn carriage which seated 22 passengers inside. There were horse-drawn stagecoaches before this, of course, both for long distances and for shorter journeys, usually with the choice of sitting inside or on the roof, but the seats required to be pre-booked at an inn; the novelty of Shillibeer's carriage was that it carried a conductor to take the fare and issue a ticket to the passenger, and the driver would stop on request to pick up and set down passengers at any convenient point. The centenary of this new service was celebrated in 1929 and a replica of Shillibeer's carriage was constructed. This is now on display in the London Transport Museum in Covent Garden, and is the first bus appearing in the following pages.

Horse-buses and the services they operated developed in London and elsewhere throughout Victorian times – seats appeared on the roof, with steps to reach them (but for men only – a Victorian lady would not climb these primitive steps and she would ride inside) and the seats upstairs could be arranged in a so-called 'knifeboard' style – a bench where you sat back-to-back – or as 'garden seats' where you sat facing forward. The oldest buses in the collection of the London Bus Museum include examples of these types, and from time to time they are run at the London Bus Museum Event Days.

The horse-bus in London was essentially a middle-class conveyance, for the fares were relatively high for the time, and the working-classes either walked or, when and where available from the second half of the Victorian Age, took a tram. A tram generally had lower fares – because the tram car was able to carry more passengers than a bus, the horses being able to pull a heavier load on rails. There are many preserved trams (including some from London) in different parts of the country, with the largest collection at the National Tramway Museum at Crich in Derbyshire, but preserved trams are not part of this book.

motor buses arrive

At the end of the 19th century the first experimental trials with mechanically-propelled buses (petrol, steam and battery electric) took place, and it was the London General Omnibus Company (LGOC) who developed the first reliable mechanically-propelled bus, the B-type of 1910, with a petrol engine. This bus proved to be so reliable in service, and was cheaper to operate than a horse-bus (horses, their feed and the necessary grooms, blacksmiths and vets were expensive), that during 1914 the last of London's horse-buses ran. The petrol-engined B-type also vanquished steam and battery electric buses, although the Tilling company persevered with its petrol-electric buses into the 1920s.

heritage
bus collections
public & private

Examples of the B-type and its larger successors – the K-type and the S-type – were retained by London General at the end of their service life as the first preserved buses. The company took the enlightened view that it was important for future generations to see how the design and appearance of the bus developed by keeping actual examples. These, and later ones preserved by London General's post-1933 statutory successor, the London Passenger Transport Board, are now to be found in the London Transport Museum collection.

This collection, and other buses added from time to time by acquisition and donation, has had several homes: as part of the Museum of British Transport (then run by the British Transport Commission, and including significant railway exhibits), it was housed in an old bus garage in Clapham during the 1960s, and later from 1973 as the London Transport Collection, the London exhibits were at Syon Park in West London. It was the foundation of the National Railway Museum at York, and the abolition of the British Transport Commission, that led to the break-up of the exhibits at Clapham.

The Collection – now the London Transport Museum – moved to the Flower Market building in Covent Garden in 1980, where it remains. The Museum is a charity and a subsidiary of Transport for London; the collection includes London underground and tube railway exhibits. There is a large depot at Acton which contains the Museum's collections not on display, and which is occasionally open to the public.

In the last 60 years or so the remains of other early London buses have also been found on farms, or elsewhere, in a derelict condition and painstakingly restored over extended periods by skilled individuals, including Mike Sutcliffe MBE and Barry Weatherhead. Some now-preserved buses have also been acquired from, or donated by, bus operators when their service life has finished. A number of examples, now in the collections of the London Transport Museum and the London Bus Museum, or retained by their restorers, can be found in the following pages.

This is the west side of Shepherd's Bush Green in early Spring 1949, looking southwards, with LT316 on the 12 route. Within a few yards this bus would turn to its left to run along Uxbridge Road before heading north to East Acton and continuing via Gypsy Corner to Willesden Junction.

RTs and RTLs took over later in the year. LT316 was new in 1931 and had a body built by Strachans, but by the time of this photograph it was carrying the body that had originally been carried by LT345.

The building with the tower was the Shepherd's Bush Empire, built in 1903. It became the BBC Television Theatre between 1953 and 1991 and since 1994 has been a music venue.

It was as late as 1956 that the first privately-preserved London bus was acquired out of service by a group of individuals. This was T31, a 1929 AEC Regal single-deck bus acquired from the LPTB's successor, the London Transport Executive, by four friends, and now in the collection of the London Bus Museum and featured in this book. One of the four, Prince Marshall, who sadly passed away at a relatively early age, took on the challenge of leading preservation efforts for a number of historic buses, some of which appear in the following pages. Two of these four pioneers – Ken Blacker and Michael Dryhurst – are still active in the historic bus preservation movement.

A list in the October 1961 issue of the magazine *Buses Illustrated* showed 76 buses known to be preserved in the UK. The number of preserved buses in the UK is now in the thousands, and over 40 London buses are in the collection of the London Bus Museum, many owned by the charity operating the Museum, the London Bus Preservation Trust, and some on long-term loan.

the London Bus Museum

The London Bus Museum is at Brooklands, near Weybridge in Surrey. The story of this museum began in 1966 when a few young men met in central London to consider how to develop their shared interest in preserving old London buses. They determined to form a group which is today the London Bus Preservation Trust, a registered charity with nearly 1,000 members, and the owner and operator of the London Bus Museum. An early priority for this group was to find premises where members' buses could be stored and where restoration work could be carried out. After a long search, the freehold of a small disused factory in Redhill Road at Cobham in Surrey was acquired. After the necessary planning permissions had been obtained and work carried out on the building, the Cobham Bus Museum, as it became known, was opened occasionally to the public from 1973.

Initially, all the buses kept there were privately owned by individuals or groups, but in due course the Cobham Bus Museum began to acquire these (and other) buses itself. The site in Redhill Road was eventually sold for redevelopment and in 2011 the collection moved to a new purpose-built facility at Brooklands, with display space for many buses and a fully-equipped workshop.

The museum was renamed the London Bus Museum. It remains the case today that, while many of the buses on display are owned by the Trust, a number continue in private ownership and are on loan to the Trust for display and use. Inevitably, the size of the collection has grown over the years and three off-site storage facilities are maintained, with buses for display periodically rotated between the Museum and off-site storage.

Many of the Museum's members volunteer their time to work on bus restorations and maintenance, and to offer their time as museum stewards, curatorial and display assistants, drivers and conductors, and in back-office roles such as finance, IT and human resources. The Museum is entirely managed and run by volunteers and has no paid staff – whether you can offer a firm commitment as a volunteer, or only assist occasionally at events, you are always welcome to talk to the Museum's officers about volunteer opportunities.

the National Association of Road Transport Museums

The NARTM represents museums and other organisations and individuals with bus collections. It has nearly 100 members and lobbies, as necessary, to ensure that these historic vehicles are still able to be used on the road and carry passengers at events, subject of course to ever-changing vehicle and driver licensing, safety and low-emissions rules. The bus preservation movement is also supported by bus operators, both large and small, who find useful publicity for their contemporary bus operations by being able to display and operate classic buses from their heritage fleets.

One of the key objectives of those owning classic buses is to display and use them in street and highway landscapes to recreate the past. To do that, we rely on those who took photographs at a time when today's preserved buses were in service. We are fortunate that there were a number of enthusiasts in the 1920s and 1930s who took photographs of London buses in street scenes, often in easily-identifiable locations where the same buildings remain today.

Two who started photographing London's buses in service from the 1940s are Alan Cross and Fred Ivey, whose names will be familiar to anyone looking at the photographic credits in any book about London's buses in the post-Second World War period. Many of their photographs have been used, with permission, to illustrate the in-service period of many of the buses shown and described in this book.

Alan B Cross

Alan Cross, born in 1931 and originally from South London, first became interested in London's buses as a young boy in the 1930s. During the Second World War, he travelled many miles by public transport to visit London's bus garages, and in so doing met other schoolboys who were similarly exploring what was to be found in those garages. At a time when information was restricted because of the war, and when there were no bus-spotter's books or lists of buses, the only way to understand the variety and composition of London's bus fleet was to see the buses for yourself, and to make notes. In due course, letters and lists of their observations began to circulate among these teenage bus enthusiasts.

It wasn't until 1944 that the first Ian Allan ABC pocket book of London Transport appeared with lists of the bus, tram and trolleybus fleets. Compiled by Barrington Tatford, the photographs in the book were either from official sources, or from the photographer W J Haynes.

Alan took his first London bus photographs using his father's camera in 1945 but it wasn't until 1948, when he bought his own first camera, that he began to be satisfied with his results.

From then until 1972 (when he moved away from London to the Midlands) Alan spent most of his spare time photographing London's bus fleet, looking to try and photograph every individual bus.

Alan had considered a career with London Transport, but in the event his working life was, firstly, with an accounting practice, and later with patent and trade mark agents. It was during this period that he took the opportunity whenever possible to acquire photographic negatives of London buses taken by photographers active in the 1920s and 1930s, including George Robbins, W Noel Jackson and J F Higham. Later, he also acquired the London bus negatives of S L Poole and Allen T Smith.

When Alan Cross started his bus photography many of London's pre-war buses in service were worn-out and life-expired but had to continue in service awaiting the arrival of the large numbers of new post-war buses on order by London Transport. Alan has always considered himself fortunate to be able to record on film the last days of the old pre-war bus fleet and the entry into service of the large numbers of new post-war buses.

For a time, from the late 1940s onwards, Alan explored the sites around London where the pre-war buses were being scrapped, taking the opportunity to make notes of individual bus numbers and locations, and acquire, when possible, the small metal plates recording the chassis number of each bus, of which he built up a big collection. It was the photographs and noting fleet, chassis and body numbers that was, and remained, Alan's principal enthusiasm, and he was not a collector of maps, timetables or other printed ephemera relating to London's buses.

Alan had long made his photographs available to collectors, attending rallies and transport sales for this purpose. He always did his own developing and printing, and generally only made his prints available to order. From 1974 he started producing a news-sheet to distribute to his customers, and this became known as *Olde Alan's Chit-Chat* and lasted until issue 59 in 1999.

These *Chit-Chats* have been collected in a book (London Bus Recollections – The Complete *Chit-Chats* of Alan Cross) published with over 70 of Alan's photographs in 2006 by the Omnibus Society. The *Chit-Chats* themselves record the inflation which took place over the period, with the price of the prints regularly increasing, together with Alan's comments and observations as a keen observer of the London bus scene over the years.

Alan has been an owner of C94 and part-owner of C111, two of the buses featured in this book – small 20-seat Leyland Cubs, both entering service in 1936. C111 was one of the eight special deck-and-a-half bodied buses, with a large luggage space at the rear; they were used on the special Inter Station bus service connecting London's main-line stations. Alan also features in another bus mentioned in this book – STL2674, but sadly this was one of the buses that did not make it into preservation.

On the left is a photograph of Alan Cross taken in 2021, while at the foot of the opposite page you can see Fred Ivey conducting a trolleybus at the East Anglia Transport Museum at Carlton Colville in 2012.

Although Alperton is on the Uxbridge branch of the Piccadilly Line, until 1932 this branch was part of the District Line. In 1931 this new station was built to the design of Charles Holden in the contemporary Moderne style.

In this view, prototype Routemaster RML3 (see pages 122-123) was parked on the forecourt. There was an electric milk float on the left with a London Transport inspector looking at it, and nearby a newsvendor's mobile cart. Just in front of the Routemaster a moped was casually parked up against the wall while a man perused the window of the estate agent. The shiny mid-1950s Humber Hawk probably belonged to a local taxi firm.

Fred Ivey

Fred Ivey was born in 1926 and, except for war service as a coal-miner in South Wales, has always lived in London and been a prolific observer and photographer of main-line trains and locomotives, London Underground trains, and London's trams, trolleybuses and buses. His career was with London Transport, starting as an Underground ticket clerk, and rising to Station Master, working for some years in that position at Uxbridge Station. His first published photograph was in 1947, of a GWR pannier tank locomotive.

In his earliest years, Fred had to move several times in the south London area and the trams of south London were his first interest and where he took his first photographs. In the post-war period, and knowing the last London trams were going to be replaced before long, he photographed many London trams and street scenes. As the trams were being replaced, Fred began to take many trolleybus pictures and with others became very active in the London trolleybus preservation movement.

The opportunity to use once a year a British Rail travel pass allowed Fred to visit Scotland on several occasions and photograph former London buses then in service with Scottish operators. Many of his photographic images were taken as slides, and Fred also took films with a cine camera, and later used a video camera. For his still images Fred Ivey only started taking digital images within the last decade, and until very recently he continued to travel around London to transport events, and to take photographs.

THE BUSES & STORIES

ST922 (featured on page 38) was photographed by Fred Ivey when it was running on tourist route 100.

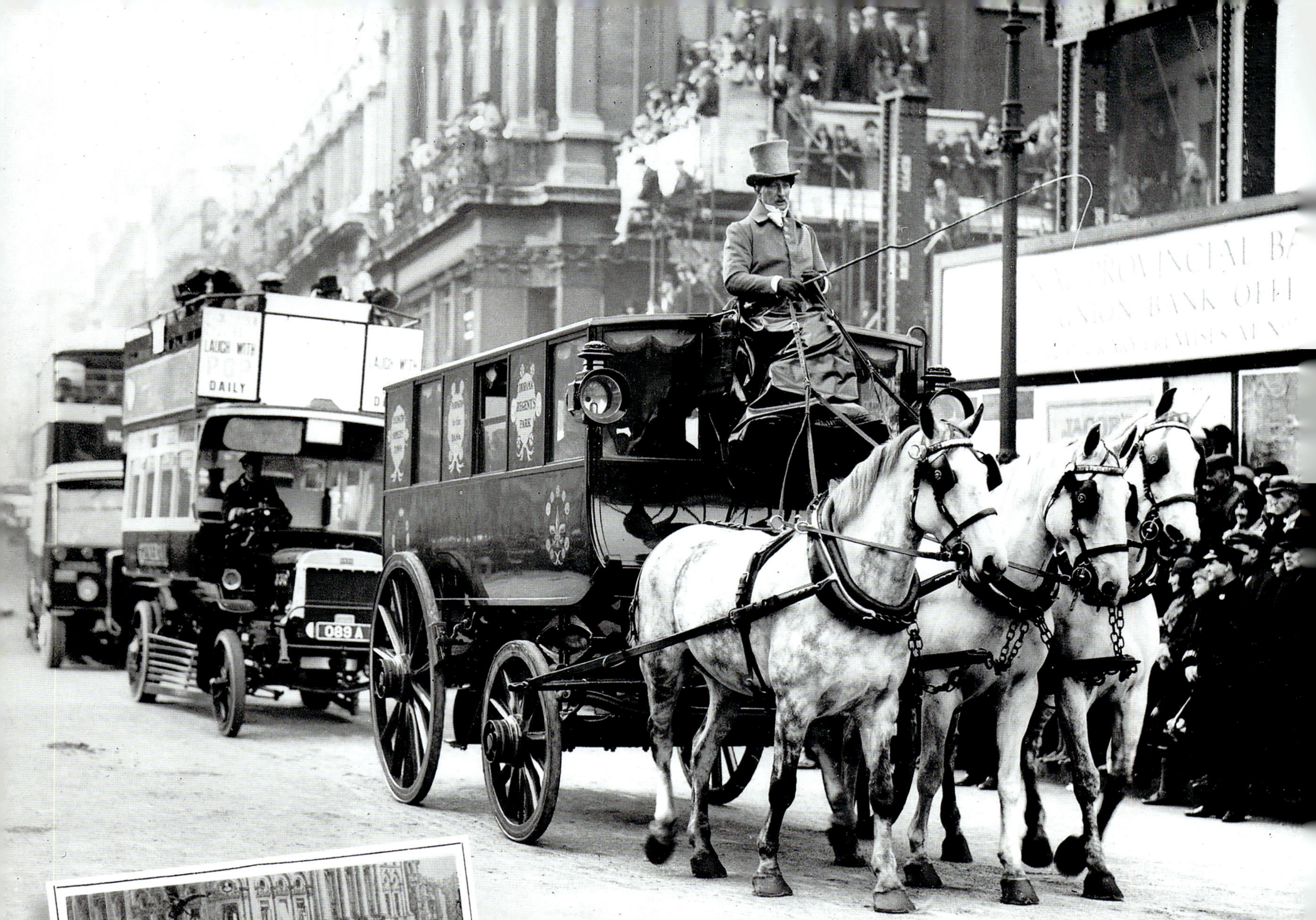
LAUGH WITH
DAILY
089 A

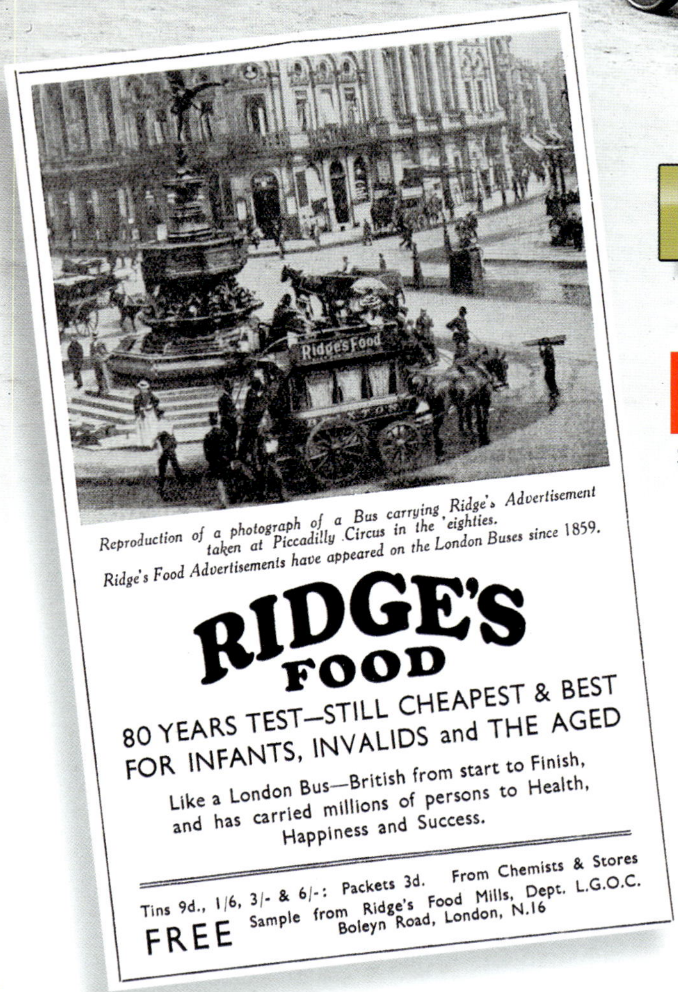
Ridges Food
Reproduction of a photograph of a Bus carrying Ridge's Advertisement taken at Piccadilly Circus in the 'eighties.
Ridge's Food Advertisements have appeared on the London Buses since 1859.
RIDGE'S
FOOD
80 YEARS TEST—STILL CHEAPEST & BEST
FOR INFANTS, INVALIDS and THE AGED
Like a London Bus—British from start to Finish, and has carried millions of persons to Health, Happiness and Success.
Tins 9d., 1/6, 3/- & 6/-: Packets 3d. From Chemists & Stores
FREE Sample from Ridge's Food Mills, Dept. L.G.O.C. Boleyn Road, London, N.16

horse buses

Following Shillibeer's horse-bus shown on the right, which was heavy and needed three horses, many competitors sprang up, often with smaller vehicles that only needed two horses, putting Shillibeer out of business.

By 1832 London had 400 horse-buses on the streets, and by the 1890s over 2,000 buses with 25,000 horses. By 1899 motorbuses were being trialled and the end for horse-buses had begun.

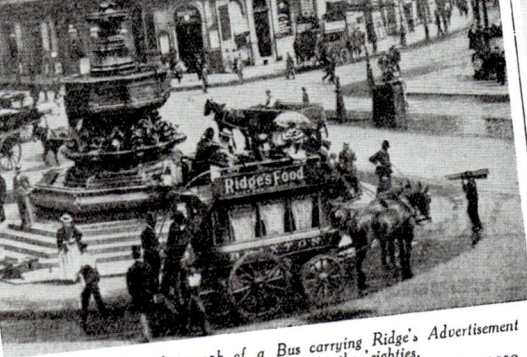

Advertisements on the inside and outside of buses have been around since these earliest times. This advert for Ridge's Food from a book published in the 1920s shows how the company was proud of its association with the London bus, showing a horse-bus by the statue of Eros in Piccadilly Circus.

Shillibeer

George Shillibeer started his omnibus service on 4 July 1829, running his three-horse 22-seat vehicle initially from Paddington Green and later from the Yorkshire Stingo pub, on the south side of the (now) Marylebone Road between Seymour Place and Sussex Gardens, to the Bank. This operation is recognised as the first true London bus service in that it picked up and set down passengers over a fixed route and at fixed times, with fares collected by a conductor as passengers left the vehicle. It was immediately copied by many rival operators to the extent that Shillibeer eventually withdrew and finished his working days as a funeral director.

The centenary of Shillibeer's enterprise was celebrated in 1929 by the London General Omnibus Company. A replica vehicle was constructed and used in the Anniversary Parade through central London. Some confusion exists over the true provenance of the replica. It is claimed for both the LGOC apprentices at Chiswick Works in West London and by Thomas Tilling Ltd at their works in Peckham. It is unlikely that, by 1929, the LGOC still had the skillsets necessary for such work, whereas Tilling was building and repairing horse-drawn commercial vehicles until the 1930s. It is recorded that the bus was driven in the Anniversary Parade by Alf Tilling, who had joined the family firm in 1877.

It was kept in store until being placed on public display at the Museum of British Transport at Clapham when it opened in 1960. In preparation for the 150th anniversary in 1979 the Shillibeer replica was completely renovated and headed a procession over the original route and, later that year, took part in the Lord Mayor's show. It is now part of the London Transport Museum collection.

On the opposite page, the Shillibeer replica was taking part in the centenary celebrations in 1929 in Whitehall.

Above is a reproduction of a contemporary print of Shillibeer's Omnibus when new.

DOOF SEGDIR

CAMBERWELL GREEN . LOUGHBORO JUNCTION
BRIXTON CHURCH . CLAPHAM.

ANDREWS STAR OMNIBUS COY LIMITED

CLAPHAM

BRIXTON

This is the 4-light knifeboard horse-bus in the London Bus Museum.

The mysterious Doof Segdir is an advertisement for Ridge's Food referred to earlier, written backwards for eye-catching effect – if if had been in mirror-writing it would have at least been legible viewed in shop windows!

Below is a coloured postcard of a 4-light, garden seat horse-bus in London service.

4-light
knifeboard

The London horse-bus evolved from Shillibeer's original concept and rapidly became an easily recognised feature on the capital's streets. The demand for passenger transport to and from the Great Exhibition in Hyde Park in 1851 led operators to add seating to the roof of their buses, giving a typical capacity of 26. Two designs of upper-deck seating layouts predominated. The example above, constructed about 1875, was called knifeboard, with seats back-to-back against a longitudinal central divider replicating the Victorian table knife holder on which the implements were cleaned and polished. 4-light refers to the number of windows on each side.

The bus was sold by London General around 1899 to the newly-formed Andrews Star Omnibus Company and used on the Clapham to Camberwell route. The bus was recovered by the Andrews family in 1963, fully overhauled, and donated to the London Bus Museum by the John Andrews Charitable Trust in 2007. It's the oldest bus in the London Bus Museum collection.

3-light
garden seat

The other, more popular, top-deck seating arrangement for horse-buses was the garden seat arrangement with pairs of seats facing forwards. This soon became the norm for motorbuses ever since.

This 3-light example on the opposite page was built by Solomon Andrews & Son around 1890 for its Star Company operating in London. After withdrawal by Star in 1909 it passed to other owners including Chessington Zoo, who used it on a service to and from Chessington South station. It was sold into private ownership in 1949 and passed through two further owners, including one in America. It returned to the UK in 1989, received an overhaul and was donated by the John Andrews Charitable Trust to the London Bus Museum in 2007.

On the left, passengers in fashions of the day were on a 3-light horse-bus in South London. By the turn of the century, the original rungs to reach the upper deck had been replaced by a staircase, and with the addition of so-called 'decency boards' a lady might now ascend to the upper deck.

Below, with a pair of fine white horses providing the power, a preserved 3-light was in use at a London Bus Museum event.

With the rapid development of the motorised passenger car came the equal application of new technology to larger vehicles, which included buses. Many and varied manufacturers tried their hand and all targeted the lucrative London market.

The established business of Leyland was one of the forerunners and in 1906 launched its Class X, of which the London Central Motor Omnibus Company was a recipient. Dimensions and layout were constrained by legislation and the insistence of the Metropolitan Police on certain exacting criteria. The original body was obtained second-hand from Thomas Tilling and, as with all buses of this era, closely resembled the horse-buses which they replaced.

LN 7270 was built in 1908 as no.14 in London Central's fleet. Later, when it was withdrawn, chassis and body were sold separately. Nothing more is known about the vehicle until the chassis was recovered from a field in Warwickshire by Mike Sutcliffe and Barry Weatherhead. Mike painstakingly restored the chassis and rebuilt a suitable body. The result, the oldest surviving British-built bus, was launched in 1996 on the annual London - Brighton Run. No.14 was included in Mike Sutcliffe's 'downsizing' sale in 2017 and was bought by the London Transport Museum together with the Chocolate Express B6 bus also featured in this book, and a 1914 Leyland Torpedo charabanc in London & North Western Railway colours.

Mike Sutcliffe, the restorer of London Central number 14, was driving the bus to take up position on display in Regent Street for the June 2014 Year of the Bus Cavalcade in the picture above.

The picture below shows three of them in earlier times with London Central.

B 43

In the picture on the right King George V was inspecting B43 and First World War veterans at Buckingham Palace in 1920.

Below, B43 was in store at the Imperial War Museum's outstation at Duxford in Cambridgeshire in November 2018 after being on loan to the London Transport Museum.

London General held back on converting its large operation to motorbuses in place of their horse-drawn predecessors. The company watched rivals experimenting with the different types on offer from manufacturers and bought several individual vehicles in order to assess their capabilities, reliability and running costs.

Following a low volume production of its own X-type, a wholesale programme followed to produce the famous B-type in the London General factory at Walthamstow. This model featured the best bits of design from all of the other tested types. The first B-type went into service in October 1910 and was followed by approximately 2,800 further examples up to 1914. They included buses in the liveries of various companies associated with the General, such as Metropolitan, Southern, National and East Surrey.

During the Great War of 1914 to 1918 some 900 B-type buses were commandeered by the military authorities, with many being shipped to France and Belgium to help with troop movements. Drivers and mechanics went with them straight out of London service. At the end of the War those buses which were worth repatriating were brought back to London and reconditioned.

In recognition of the contribution made by London busmen to the war effort, King George V requested that he inspect representatives. B43 was provided with a body from store, which was in better condition than its original, and was presented to His Majesty at Buckingham Palace in February 1920. It was kept as a mobile war memorial by London General and subsequently passed to the Auxiliary Omnibus Companies Association, and later moved into the Imperial War Museum, in whose care it remains.

It was given the sobriquet *Ole Bill* by war veterans after the famous war-time cartoon character created by Captain Charles Bruce Bairnsfather, which had appeared in *The Bystander* magazine. A representation of Ole Bill himself, in bronze, was affixed to the bus radiator. While on loan to the London Transport Museum it was presented together with B340, B1609 and B2737 on Covent Garden Piazza in September 2018, thus, probably uniquely, displaying the four remaining complete B-type buses in one place.

B2737

On 27 September 2014, marking 100 years since the start of the First World War, B2737 was taken to the Somme *departement* in northern France, and in the picture below was posed in front of the famous Thiepval War Memorial.

A month earlier, on 29 August, this bus was re-enacting old times on route 9 (Barnes - Liverpool Street), shown on the opposite page alongside much more modern buses with St Paul's Cathedral in the background.

To commemorate the contribution made by London General and its drivers and mechanics, the London Transport Museum reconstructed a B-type motorbus using components from various sources, including the chassis, which research revealed was, without doubt, that of B2737. The work was carried out by Richard Peskett and the project directed by Tim Shields. The complete bus was ready to be launched in full London General colours in June 2014 and was exhibited at a number of venues during that Year of the Bus.

This was followed by the repainting of the bus, symbolically in full public view, into wartime khaki green. Alterations were made, which included the boarding up of the lower deck windows, thus replicating the condition in which some 900 similar buses were used in France and Belgium during the First World War to convey troops and in use for other roles.

In September 2014 the bus was taken on the Battlebus tour of battlefields, cemeteries, towns and memorials in the Ypres and Somme areas, to much acclaim. A subsequent trip was made in 2016 as part of the Battle of the Somme commemorations. On return it has been demonstrated at many events across the UK and has assisted in educational projects. It is currently on display in the London Transport Museum at Covent Garden.

The Thiepval Memorial to the Missing of the Somme, near the village of Thiepval in Picardy in France, was designed by the notable English architect Sir Edwin Lutyens for the Imperial War Graves Commission. It was built between 1928 and 1932 and its simple, powerful form rises elegantly 140 feet above the level of its podium.

The Portland stone piers are engraved with the names of the 72,246 officers and men known to have lost their lives in the Somme battles between July 1915 and March 1918 and who have no known grave. Over 90% of these soldiers died in the first Battle of the Somme between 1 July and 18 November 1916, a shocking statistic.

The first 1:32 scale Airfix plastic construction kit of the B-type appeared in 1962; the First World War military version in 1966.

K 502

K502 represents London General's next major bus design after the famous B-type.

Four years of war had put a stop on any development of London General's motorbus fleet, and the loss of so many B-types for military service had led to widespread cuts in bus services, not to mention frustration on the part of London's bus users. So it wasn't until 1919 that the K-type appeared, but it did represent a major change in design and layout. The driver and engine were now placed side-by-side, the top deck extended and, in consequence, seating capacity increased from the B-type's 34 to 46. This basic layout was to remain the standard for London right through to the last Routemaster built in 1968.

A total of over 1,150 K-types were built, some single deck, with the last entering service in 1926. A number of external body-builders were contracted by London General in order to keep up with the production of chassis. These included Brush of Loughborough, Dodson and Strachan, both of London, and Short Brothers of Rochester in Kent.

All K-types had been withdrawn by early 1931, except for 10 which had to be kept for a while because of a weight restriction on Chertsey Bridge. After withdrawal, London General rapidly sold off its K-types rather than scrapping them – some went complete to other bus operators, both at home and abroad, and many went to private individuals for use as holiday homes near the seaside. Some of the wooden bodies went at £5 a time for conversion into garden sheds and summerhouses, and some to pig and chicken farmers for the luxury accommodation of their animals!

Barry Weatherhead has been a much-respected restorer of old vehicles – cars and lorries, as well as London buses – since the mid-1960s. His initial enthusiasm was for steam-driven vehicles but he chanced across the remains of K502 in a hedge while negotiating the purchase of a traction engine. He was told he could have the bus for £5, so long as he took it away soon, otherwise it would be broken up.

This bus had been sold by London General in 1930 to George Cohen, the scrap dealer, and resold for use as a hen house on a chicken farm in Orwell, Suffolk, along with 196 others! The engine, gearbox, differential and other bits were missing, but Barry eventually found or made what was required. The engine came from a scrapyard in Shaftesbury in Dorset and the propshaft and other pieces from another K-type which had found its way to a smallholding halfway up a mountainside in North Wales!

After nine years' work, the bus was ready to complete the HCVC London – Brighton Run in 1975 and now complements K424, which was kept by London General and resides in the London Transport Museum collection.

We couldn't find a photograph of K502 in original London service, but what could be better than the view on this page of a K-type in 1926, well-loaded and with everyone wearing a hat.

It was coming round Parliament Square with Broad Sanctuary leading to Victoria Street heading off on the left. You can make out the dome of Westminster Central Hall, too.

Cochran's Revue was at the London Pavilion in Piccadilly Circus and ran from 29 April to 4 September with 148 performances.

S 454

The S-type was London General's next development after the K-type, and the first example entered service in January 1921. By then the maximum weight allowance had been increased to 8 tons and this allowed 54 seats to be installed. Like the K-type, the S-type had an ash frame with metal flitch plates, but the engine output had been increased from 28 to 35 horsepower to cope with the extra weight. It also had larger wheels.

Although pneumatic tyres were later fitted to most of the S-types, including all of the single-deck versions, Metropolitan Police regulations still forbade an enclosed top deck or driver's cab. The single-deckers later received full cabs and windscreens.

Double-deck S-types were withdrawn by 1931 but, luckily, two examples remain with us. S742 was placed in the London Transport Collection straight from service and at the time of writing was on loan to the British Motor Museum at Gaydon in Warwickshire.

In the picture below, S616 was passing through Watford Market Place in February 1927.

On the right, preserved S454 was passing through Staplefield in Sussex on its way to Brighton in May 2018.

S454, new in October 1922, was sold in April 1931 to a dealer. It passed through a couple of owners subsequently, but by 1964 was laid up in a breaker's yard near Tring in Hertfordshire. It was rescued by Michael Banfield and completely rebuilt. Although the frames and mechanical components were reusable, the bodywork was in a very poor state and could only be used to provide templates for a replacement. The bus was finished within a remarkable three years and was then entered for the London - Brighton Run in 1968.

After Michael Banfield's death, his large collection of vehicles, parts and ephemera was auctioned in 2014. S454 was acquired by a private collector, as was Michael Banfield's 1922 Tilling-Stevens petrol-electric double-decker, described on the following page. One or other of these historic buses is usually on loan to the London Bus Museum.

The stage play The Constant Nymph (from the 1924 book by Margaret Kennedy) was being advertised on the side of S616. It opened on 14 September 1926 at New Theatre in London's St Martin's Lane and ran for nearly a year before going on tour.

Preserved 935 was photographed at Staplefield in Sussex on its way to Brighton in May 2018.

Early motor buses were built to varying specifications at the whim of each manufacturer. Control positions varied and most vehicles with a petrol engine transmitted power to the rear wheels via a clutch, gearbox and differential. These controls were cumbersome to operate and drivers often contributed to clutch and gearbox failures by inappropriate use of the associated levers and pedals. There was an alternative.

Thomas Tilling introduced petrol-electric buses to London in 1908. They had a petrol engine which drove a dynamo that fed power to an electric motor, rather than through a clutch and gearbox direct to the rear axle. This was an attempt to make it easier for the early drivers, especially those transferring from trams, to manage the controls and provided a much smoother ride without the need to operate a clutch mechanism. The electrical equipment was provided by Messrs W A Stevens of Maidstone and the buses were completed in Tilling's own works in Peckham.

A double-deck example of a Tilling-Stevens petrol-electric bus has survived thanks to the rescue carried out by the late Michael Banfield in 1970. The bus was delivered to Tilling's in June 1922 on which it built a body constructed on the trussed-girder principle for extra strength. It remained in service until 1931 when it was sold to a dealer in Bethnal Green.

Michael Banfield, who was then chairman of the Historic Commercial Vehicle Club, acquired it from a scrapyard and carried out restoration work which involved using original panels, framework and roof as templates because of their deteriorated condition. Most of the fittings and the engine were reusable and, after many years' work, it emerged from the workshops in 2008.

As already mentioned, Michael Banfield's collection was auctioned in 2014. As with S454, XL 1204 was acquired by a private collector, each bus selling for over £200,000.

A similar chassis, including engine and generator, is held in the London Transport Museum collection. This had been new to Douglas Corporation on the Isle of Man, but the body was removed in 1938 when the chassis became a mobile generator.

keeping it going 1

Tree Lopper 971J in the picture on the right was converted from AEC Regent double-decker STL1470 built in 1936. Most of the front-entrance bus body survived with just the top deck modified to allow gangs to cut back overhanging branches which were liable to damage service buses. It was bought from a private owner for preservation in 1973 and, after many years' work, is now fully restored.

Breakdown tender 738J shown below is privately owned, but is on display at the London Bus Museum. It uses the chassis, engine, etc. from 1933-built bus STL169 with a new van body built in 1950 for use in heavy recovery situations. It was sold out of service in 1971. While in preservation, the body was largely destroyed by arsonists but a replacement replica was built.

Most bus and coach operators have a need for ancillary vehicles which enable important back-up tasks to be performed. These might range from a single service van to fetch and carry tools and equipment for breakdowns, through to many hundreds of vehicles for a whole range of specialist tasks.

London Transport operations required support in many forms and it maintained a fleet of cars, vans and lorries to provide transport for staff, tools and equipment and many other sundry items between its various works and garages/depots.

Additionally, many specialist vehicles were required and these included those converted from old buses, such as heavy recovery, overhead line repair to tram and trolleybus wires, tree cutting, mobile staff canteens, food delivery to canteens at works and garages and even coaches converted to ambulances for evacuation purposes during the Second World War.

Understandably, these ancillary vehicles did not attract much attention from preservationists when efforts were concentrated on complete buses. Some exceptions survive, particularly where the original bus was converted to some other role and only the chassis remained as built.

In this picture
Chocolate Express B6 was rounding
Parliament Square in the Year of the Bus Cavalcade in June 2014.

On the opposite page it was in Trafalgar Square in the 1920s with the National
Gallery in the background and the statue of General Sir Charles James Napier
behind the bus.

The 1920s saw a remarkable upsurge in competition by the so-called 'pirate' bus operators against the established concerns, principally the London General Omnibus Company. London General's fleet had developed slowly and carefully, but its buses were rather old-fashioned by comparison and passenger comfort had suffered as a result.

Following the rapid improvements in heavy vehicle design, spurred on by the demand during the First World War, companies such as Leyland, Dennis and Guy were able to offer buses and lorries which were faster and increasingly more reliable. These appealed strongly to such entrepreneurs as Arthur Partridge, who had started his Chocolate Express Omnibus Company in 1922, following a spell as a London taxi driver.

Leyland XU 7498 was his fourth vehicle and was to Leyland's latest LB5 specification. It went on the road on 3 December 1924, initially on solid tyres, but was upgraded to pneumatics in 1930. The advent of the London Passenger Transport Board in July 1933, with its compulsory powers of purchase of all omnibus operators in its wide London area, saw Partridge's operation pass to the Board in August 1934. Although the LPTB continued to operate XU 7498 for a short while, it was sold later that same month to a showman.

At some stage the body was separated from its chassis and was discovered by well-known early Leyland restorer, Mike Sutcliffe, on a farm in Norfolk. Mike recovered the body and set about finding a suitable chassis and other mechanical parts to enable a full restoration to begin. Mike recounts the long story of this in his book, *The Leyland Man*. The complete and immaculate bus was finished in time to take part in the 1987 London - Brighton Run.

Little Lectures by Nurse Wincarnis. Lecture No. 4

Nerve Troubles.

Our nerves are like an intricate network of telegraph wires. They are controlled and nourished by a portion of the brain known as the nerve centres. The condition of the nerve centres depends upon the condition of the bodily health. When the bodily health is lowered the nerves suffer in sympathy. Then it is that we are tormented with "nerves," headaches, neuralgia, and nervous debility. In such cases there is nothing to equal "Wincarnis," the "Wine of Life." "Wincarnis" is a powerful nerve food which acts directly upon the nerve centres and gives them new life and new vitality. The result is wonderful.

WINCARNIS

Small Size. 3/- All Wine Merchants, Licensed Chemists & Grocers Large sell Wincarnis. Will you try just One Bottle? Size. 5/-

"WINCARNIS" IS RECOMMENDED BY OVER 10,000 DOCTORS.

This once very popular fortified tonic wine was being advertised on the side of the bus in the picture above. It tasted not unlike sweet sherry and was claimed to have all sorts of restorative powers for nervous problems and tiredness.

D 142

The 1925 Dennis in the collection of the London Bus Museum represents the activities of some of the earliest enthusiast bus rescuers and restorers. It was a youthful Prince Marshall who discovered this bus at Wickford in Essex in 1971, covered in corrugated iron and being used as a store shed.

XX 9591 is a 4-ton Dennis with a body by Dodson with 48 seats, 26 on the upper deck and 22 on the lower deck. It was delivered in April 1925 to William Cook, one of London's independent bus operators, which were then usually called 'pirates'. Cook traded as Dominion, using this bus, and another similar, on route 514, which ran from Shepherd's Bush to Hayes along the Uxbridge Road. But the next year, 1926, Cook's business and his buses were acquired by London General. These buses were sold on by London General to Redburn's Motor Services, which was taken over by the London Public Omnibus Company Limited, a well-funded independent operator which was buying up competitors' businesses.

By 1928 Public had acquired over 200 buses and it became known that Public was being financed by London General and was fully absorbed by it in 1929. This brought XX 9591 into London General ownership once more. The bus was disposed of in 1932, eventually being discovered in Essex.

Under Prince Marshall's direction, the bus was restored and subsequently had an active life. In 1977 it made a sponsored tour to Japan, and has toured in much of England. For a time from 1980 the bus was operated commercially on route 100, a tourist route in Central London operated by the Obsolete Fleet company. The London Bus Museum acquired the bus in 1984 and since then it has been used extensively at heritage transport events, the City of London Lord Mayor's Show, and for television and film work.

Below, XX 9591 was on route 514 on the Uxbridge Road in West Ealing heading westwards for Hayes just before the junction with Northfield Avenue.

The bus was hand-painted into a blue livery by an outside specialist, but most of the rest of the body and mechanical refurbishment and restoration was done by volunteer members of the Museum in the well-equipped workshop of the London Bus Museum, situated next to the Museum building itself at Brooklands.

By 2020 it was clear that another major refurbishment of the body and chassis was necessary to keep the vehicle in good operating condition, and it moved into the Museum's own workshop for work to be done. The livery worn by the bus in original Cook/Dominion days was red, and that was also the livery in which it ran for London General, and in which it was first restored.

However, for the latest refurbishment the bus has been expertly repainted into the blue livery in which it ran for Public between 1928 and 1932. In this livery it was re-launched to the public in October 2022 at the London Bus Museum's annual October TransportFest event at Brooklands, and it is once more a major attraction in the Bus Museum's fleet of operating heritage buses.

keeping it going 2

In the picture above, Tower Wagon 89Q was being demonstrated at the London Bus Museum's event at Brooklands in October 2017.

The picture above right shows London Bus Museum's mobile canteen unit before it was fully restored.

In the main picture below, 89Q was crossing the bridge over the railway at Leyton Station on the Central Line in June 1961.

While the economical reuse of redundant bus chassis was widespread within London Transport, many requirements had to be met with conventional commercially-available lorries. Even so, there were some unusual vehicles. The extensive tram and trolleybus network required specialist vehicles for use by maintenance gangs. LT bought a fleet of AEC lorry chassis in the 1930s which had extending towers powered through the lorry's transmission. The London Transport Museum acquired tower wagon 89Q in 1985, following its use by a garage for vehicle recovery, and restored it with a fully-working replica tower.

London Transport was a prolific user of Bedfords from the 1950s until allegiance switched to Ford in the 1960s. Interesting were 10 Bedford prime-movers with a fleet of 13 mobile canteen trailers. These replaced converted AEC Regent ST-type buses such as ST922 (see pages 38-39).

In due course, Liverpool Corporation Transport acquired certain of these prime-movers and trailers from London Transport, and after Liverpool had retired these units, in 1973 Bedford OSS prime-mover JXC 2 (once 702B in London Transport's service fleet numbering system) together with semi-trailer MC11 arrived at the London Bus Museum. Both tractor unit and canteen semi-trailer have been restored by Museum volunteers back to original London Transport condition.

O172

Above is O172 as reconstructed by Barry Weatherhead.

Below is the only known image of O172 in service. Although neither registration nor fleet numbers are visible, it is known that Tilling's buses ran daily with the same running number, with only infrequent changes. O172 ran as 4 TB from Bromley garage.

Preserved O172 in the picture above is a Tilling-Stevens TS7 petrol electric bus built in October 1925, one of 12 identical single-deckers with 30-seat rear-entrance bodywork built by London General for its associate, Thomas Tilling. It went into service from Tilling's Bromley garage on local route 109 between Penge and Bromley, which involved going through the Chislehurst Arch. This well-known landmark was a water tower spanning the roadway.

Initially it was in General livery. In 1930 it gained pneumatic tyres and was later relicensed in Tilling's colours. Withdrawn in 1932, this bus was sold to a showman at Godstone in Surrey for use on fairgrounds, for which its electric dynamo proved invaluable. It was rescued by Barry Weatherhead and restored over a period of ten years, which included locating an authentic engine, dynamo and electric motor. A replacement radiator had to be constructed using original drawings.

NS 1995

London General's NS-type was the company's next incarnation of home-designed and built motor buses for its extensive London operations. Taking advantage of new technology, the NS had a drop-frame chassis which allowed a lower floor and platform height. Although this resulted in a lower centre of gravity, the Metropolitan Police would still not allow a roof to be fitted because of concerns about buses overturning. It has been claimed that NS stood for Nulli Secundus (Second to None), or perhaps 'no step'?

Over 1,700 were built, and from 1925 top deck covers and, later, enclosed driver's cabs and pneumatic tyres, were allowed, and were retro-fitted, too.

NS1995 was new to Forest Gate garage in 1927 and withdrawn in 1937. London Transport kept the bus in its museum collection, eventually residing at Acton Depot, but rarely seen on the road due to concerns over its rear tyres. These are of an obsolete size and, were replacements ever needed, acquisition would involve very expensive one-off manufacture, even assuming that a source could be found.

Only one other NS is known to still exist. This is NS174 of 1923, which has been in the process of reconstruction by volunteers at the London Bus Museum. Much of the body is of new construction, but original parts have been utilised where possible.

When completed in its original form with solid tyres, no roof and no driver's cab, it will make an interesting comparison with NS1995, an example of the NS-class bus in the form in which it was finally withdrawn from service.

The reconstruction of NS174 has been taking place in the public area of the Bus Museum, to allow visitors to see something of the work involved. At the time of writing, it is intended that completion should be by 2024.

On the opposite page preserved NS1995 was on its way to the Year of the Bus display in Regent Street in 2014.

Unfortunately, no image of NS1995 is service has come to light. The official picture below is of a similar vehicle, NS2154.

Above is the London Bus Museum's NS174 undergoing restoration in mid-2022.

Originally, in America, Force wheat-based breakfast cereal was sold in a box decorated with images of muscular men wrestling with chains. But it didn't sell well.

Then in 1901 the character of Sunny Jim was invented, an advertising campaign launched and by 1904 one factory had expanded to several and 360,000 packets were being manufactured every day. It was also launched in the UK.

It reached its peak popularity in 1930, selling 12.5 million packets, but over the years sales declined and by 2013, now a UK only product, it was no more.

T 31

By the end of the 1920s bus chassis manufacturer AEC had three new, much-improved models available, built at its modern factory at Southall. These were the 6-wheel Renown and shorter 4-wheel Regent double-deckers, and the 4-wheel single-deck Regal. The London General Omnibus Company would standardise on these types for its ambitious programme of fleet renewal as the LT-class (Renown), ST-class (Regent) and T-class (Regal), and, after the London Passenger Transport Board was formed in 1933, London Transport continued with the Regent and Regal as its standard types.

Although prototypes LT1 and ST1 had already appeared, 10 T-class Regals entered service with little fanfare in December 1929 in London's eastern suburbs. This was the start of a class of single-deckers that was added to over the following two decades, with nearly 800 constructed or acquired by London General and London Transport, and the last not leaving the fleet until the early 1960s (see pages 82-3).

T31's body was built by London General in its Chiswick Works and was one of the first batch of 50. It entered service from Nunhead garage on local circular route 621, but later operated from several different garages through to 1952, when it became a driver-trainer and staff bus. It outlasted its fellows as it was allocated to Chiswick for use within the works before finally being sold out of store from Norbiton garage.

T31 is acknowledged as the first historic London bus to be restored by private individuals in the UK. It was bought for £45 direct from London Transport in 1956 and led a nomadic existence while the group attempted to find a home which would allow undercover restoration to be undertaken. It formed the nucleus of what became the London Bus Preservation Trust.

The rebuild included restoration of its original rear-entrance with open platform, concealed interior lighting and reconversion to petrol engine.

It has been owned by the London Bus Museum since 1994, the purchase aided by a grant from the Science Museum's Prism Fund.

In the picture above, T31 was arriving at Brighton's Madeira Drive on the HCVS Run in May 2016.

During its time at Chiswick it was used as a driver-trainer and was showing its L-plates in the picture on the left.

The bottom picture on this page shows T31 parked at an outdoor location in Worthing during its lengthy restoration. The original rear entrance had been restored by this time.

On the opposite page, T31 was photographed at Worcester Park Station in September 1949.

ST 922

Restored as Tilling 6098, this bus was at the Worshipful Company of Carmen's Cart Marking ceremony at the City of London's Guildhall on 18 July 2018 in the picture above.

On the left is a view inside the downstairs section looking forwards when it was in use as a canteen.

As mobile canteen, 693J was photographed in Morden Hall Road in August 1950 ready to provide food and drink to Derby Day bus crews.

Thomas Tilling was born in 1825 and graduated from running a dairy business in Walworth to operating horses and carriages for hire. His first horse-bus ran in 1849 over the route between Peckham and Oxford Street. His organisation grew rapidly and by the height of the horse-bus era he owned 7,000 horses and 250 buses. He contracted to supply transport for many non-passenger organisations, including the Royal Mail and several national newspapers.

The advent of the motorbus saw the Tilling family (Thomas Tilling died in 1893) engaged in early experiments and included the construction of bus bodies in its own workshops in Peckham. A revenue-sharing agreement on specific routes between London General and Tilling's included the supply of buses by the former. This involved taking advantage of London General's favourable relationship with AEC, so in 1930 an order was placed for 136 Regent chassis to be bodied by Tilling.

Some of these buses were intended for Tilling's operations in the Brighton area. Fleet number 6098 was part of this Brighton batch but was delivered to Tilling's Catford garage in November 1930 for use on local routes instead.

On the takeover of Tilling's buses by London Transport in 1933 it was numbered ST922 in sequence with London General's large fleet of AEC Regents. It was loaned to Midland Red in Birmingham between 1941 and 1943 to assist with temporary replacement of war-damaged buses. When it was returned to London it worked from Putney (Chelverton Road) garage until being withdrawn at the end of 1946. It was then converted into a mobile canteen. Mobile canteens were located at strategic points around London to provide food and drinks to bus crews at remote terminals.

The bus was sold in 1955 and, after a spell with British Road Services at Tufnell Park, probably as a static office, it went to dealer, Rush Green Motors at Codicote in Hertfordshire, from where it was rescued by Prince Marshall in 1966. It was rebuilt and recertified for use in Prince's Obsolete Fleet operation, running up to 10 hours each day on sightseeing route 100. The bus was acquired by the London Bus Museum in 1984 and restored to Tilling's livery in 2019.

LT165

Ever since the earliest legislation covering horse-drawn vehicles, buses and other commercial vehicles have been restricted in carrying capacity by virtue of the maximum weight allowed per axle. So when revised legislation permitted a longer bus, placing the chassis on three axles instead of the customary two enabled more passengers to be carried.

London's LT-type on the AEC Renown chassis was introduced in 1929 and allowed 60 seated passengers, although it was not the first three-axle bus to be constructed. The early LTs featured outside staircases, but from the 151st example, LT-class double-deckers were built with enclosed stairs. A total of 1,325 LTs were built, which included 199 single-deckers.

LT165 is the only survivor of the double-deck version by virtue of being retained by London Transport for its historic vehicle collection after it was withdrawn from service in 1949. Having been on public display successively at the Clapham Museum of Transport, then at Syon Park London Transport Collection, it then became part of the London Transport Museum fleet and has been kept at Acton Depot.

Although it was taken to Regent Street for the Year of the Bus event in June 2014, it had to be towed there and back because of a defective engine. The engine has been under overhaul, but this task proved to be a challenge, because it was discovered that the diesel engine fitted in 1938 may well have been replaced during the Second World War by a non-standard unit and certain important parts have had to be specially manufactured.

On the left, LT165 was at Brixton in July 1949 on the high-frequency 35 route. LTs from Leyton garage worked this route alongside STLs through most of the 1940s.

In its preserved state, LT 165 was posed at Kew Pumping Station on 19 June 2010 in the picture on the opposite page.

Opened by the Grand Junction Waterworks Company in 1838, Kew Bridge Pumping Station replaced an earlier one at Chelsea due to poor water quality. It eventually housed six steam pumping engines, as well as four Allen diesel pumps and four electric pumps. Although the steam engines were retired in 1944, two were kept on standby until 1958

The Kew Bridge Engines Trust, a registered charity, was formed in 1974 and the site has been described as *"the most important historic site of the water supply industry in Britain."*

LT1059

As well as the double-deck AEC Renowns in the LT-type family, London General commissioned 199 single-deck versions to replace various obsolete buses then being used on routes requiring high-capacity single-deckers. The entrance doorway on these was at the front behind the front wheel, rather than at the back, as on the vehicles being replaced. Bizarrely, the Metropolitan Police forbade doors being placed on London buses at this time (and indeed right through to the 1952 red Central Area RF-type), although their Country Area versions did have doors controlled by the conductor, and later by the driver when one-person operation was allowed. Almost all of the single-deck LTs were always painted red for Central Area work and were nicknamed Scooters by their crews.

Together with a host of obsolete buses which had had to be kept going immediately after the war while waiting for new replacement vehicles, the last single-deck LTs didn't finally leave public service until 1953. At that time, old buses were eagerly sought after for use as cheap accommodation for holiday use and sometimes even for permanent residence, and two single-deck LTs were recovered after such use.

LT1076 was rescued around 1980 and subsequently rebuilt by the London Transport Museum. Similar vehicle LT1059 escaped from use as a caravan at Teignmouth in Devon in 1970. Having been in private hands for several years, it became part of the London Bus Museum collection and joined the restoration queue, despite much of the bodywork having disappeared over time.

In June 2019 the London Bus Museum pulled out all the stops and gathered together as many of the Trust's vehicles as it could for the annual Summer on the Buses event. One bus awaiting its place in the restoration queue was 1931 AEC Renown single-decker LT1059.

This remains in the state in which it was recovered many years ago and for which large amounts of time and money will be required for its restoration. By invitation, the London Transport Museum provided stablemate LT1076 which was fully restored following acquisition in 1994.

Above are the two LT single-deckers together and on the right LT1059 with the tarpaulin raised to give an indication of the amount of work to be done.

Single-deck
LT1008 was based at
Dalston garage (code D) working the
208A route when the photograph above
was taken on 25 June 1952.

This route was introduced in 1941,
running between Clapton Pond, Hackney
Wick, Stratford and Maryland. RFs took
over in 1952 and in May 1959 the route
was renumbered 178 and lowbridge
bodied RLH types were allocated to
cope with increased passenger loadings
(see pages 102-103).

Three years before this photograph was
taken, LT1008's life had been extended
with a thorough rebuild by Marshall's
of Cambridge, and it received a diesel
engine transplanted from an STL which,
luckily, was short enough to fit within
the existing engine compartment

Behind the LT was a side-engined AEC
Q on the 208. This route ran between
Clapton Pond, Hackney Wick and
Bromley-by-Bow. One of the other
variations of the Q-class is dealt with
on pages 48-49.

In the lower picture on the right,
LT1059 was in Wood Street yard in
Kingston in 1949. It's interesting to
compare the original detailing on this
LT with the rebuilt version in the
picture above.

trolleybuses

Trolleybuses were electrically powered from overhead wires and renowned for their rapid acceleration and near-silent running.

For much of its existence, the London trolleybus system was the largest in the world. At its zenith, there were 68 routes and at one time it was run with 1,811 trolleybuses. However, in 1954 it was announced that all trolleybuses were to be replaced by diesel buses. The system was closed in stages, the first in 1959, a§§§§nd the final trolleybus day was 8 May 1962.

However, the route was so thronged with sightseers, enthusiasts and people trying to board, that the final trolleybus didn't arrive back at the depot until the early hours of 9 May. Fulwell depot operated both the very first and very last trolleybus in London.

Incidentally, trolleybuses and trams ran out of depots, and buses out of garages, in London Transport parlance.

London United Tramways, part of the Underground group from 1913, bought a fleet of 60 trolleybuses for tram replacement and for route development, based on Kingston and Wimbledon in Surrey. These operated out of Fulwell depot and began running on 16 May 1931. The initial batch of trolleys were designated as classes A1 and A2 and given the unofficial name Diddlers by the staff, although the reason for adoption of the name has been lost.

The Diddlers were replaced in 1948 by a new generation of trolleybus, but no.1 was kept for preservation by London Transport. It was taken out from the Museum of British Transport at Clapham for a ceremonial tour over the remaining sections of trolleybus routes from Fulwell on 8 May 1962, the last day of London Transport trolleybus operation. It was returned to Museum stock, but in 1975 taken to London Transport's Aldenham Works for repairs and repainting. It was later placed in London Transport Museum's Acton Depot in a rather frail state in terms of wiring and bodywork. However, it was coaxed back into life for exhibition and demonstration runs at the East Anglia Transport Museum on the 50th anniversary of the closure of the London system in May 2012.

Below, trolleybus 1 was at Fulwell depot on 8 May 1962, the last day of London trolleybuses.

50 years later, in the picture at the bottom of the opposite page, it was photographed at the East Anglia Transport Museum in May 2012 to commemorate the 50th anniversary of the end of London trolleybuses.

STL 441

By the mid-1930s the layout of the double-deck bus, not only in London, but across the UK, had become established as a result of legislation and perceived best practice. It had evolved typically into a two-axle vehicle (with exceptions – see the LT-type and London trolleybuses) with a rear open platform, enclosed staircase and driver's cab, seating between 50 and 60 passengers and powered by a diesel engine.

London General's and London Transport's strong links with AEC meant that AEC's range of passenger chassis was developed primarily for London use. The Regent chassis was introduced in 1929 and remained in production until the 1960s, albeit with improved specifications as the years went on. London General and London Transport took a large number of the lengthened STL-type from 1932 and these were allocated not only to both the Central and Country Areas but also to the associated fleet of Tilling's.

Although ordered by London General, STL441 was delivered after the formation of London Transport in May 1934, with a body built in London Transport's own works at Chiswick. Originally it had a petrol engine, but this was replaced by a 7.7-litre diesel in May 1939. The body had to be raised at the front to accommodate this larger engine, causing these re-engined STLs to be described as 'leaning back'. In January 1948 this bus was sent to Mann Egerton in Norwich for body restoration work to keep it going for a few more years until being withdrawn in 1952. Its last garage allocation was Streatham.

STL441 has the lowest bonnet number of several restored STL-type London buses and has an interesting history. By special request it was sold direct to the Instituut voor den Autohandel in the Netherlands in 1953. The Instituut was a training organisation for the Dutch transport industry and wanted a bus for its museum collection. However, the STL remained untouched and began to deteriorate until rescued and acquired by the London Bus Preservation Trust in 1974. Similar vehicle STL469 is part of the London Transport Museum collection.

On the opposite page STL441 was shifting the crowds at Morden Station on 16 April 1952, not long before withdrawal.

Above, in its preserved state it was posed on Ludgate Hill in February 2018. Only the modern shops really give the game away!

The picture on the right shows STL441 in service on the 14A. This ran from Hornsey Rise by way of King's Cross, Piccadilly Circus, Knightsbridge and South Kensington to Putney, Kingston and Hampton Court.

Since the earliest days, manufacturers have experimented to find the best place to position the engine.

AEC engineers were impressed by an American design which placed the engine on the offside behind the driver, and tilted over so it could fit under the offside seats. This revolutionary concept enabled the number of seats on a UK single-decker to be increased to 35. Some double-deck Q-types were also built but did not find favour.

Following an initial experimental vehicle built for London General in 1932, London Transport bought 232 further examples. There were red front-entrance Central Area buses and centre-entrance Green Line coaches, both with Park Royal bodies, though to slightly differing styles, as well as the centre-entrance Country Area buses bodied by the Birmingham Railway Carriage & Wagon Company, as shown by Q83 on these pages.

Q83 was delivered in October 1935 as a Country bus at Dorking garage. It was converted for Green Line work in 1936 with heaters, luggage racks and roof boards added, but two years later it was back to being a bus. It ended its days with London Transport at Northfleet garage in 1954 and was then sold to the Sutton Coldfield Old People's Welfare Committee. A ramp was added to the rear of the bus to provide access for those using wheelchairs.

The bus was bought for preservation in 1966 and acquired by the London Bus Museum in 2003. Having previously been restored in Central Area red livery, which it never carried in service but representing many others which did, Q83 was painted in pre-war Green Line colours in 2018.

Only one other London Q-type is known to survive, Q55. This was withdrawn from service in October 1953 and transferred to London Transport Museum stock. It was brought out of store at Acton Depot to be displayed alongside Q83 at a Brooklands event in 2015.

In the big picture on the opposite page Q83 was photographed on the Historic Commercial Vehicle Society London to Brighton Run in May 2018.

Below that, Q83 (in red livery) was alongside Q55 in October 2015 at the London Bus Museum's TransportFest event.

In the picture at the top of this page Q83 was loading up in St Albans on 16 April 1949 on the 355 route.

The picture on the left shows Q83 while it was owned by Sutton Coldfield Old People's Welfare Committee.

C94

In the picture above, C94 was arriving at the 'lost' village of Imber on Salisbury Plain on 21 August 2021 as London Transport Museum's contribution to the annual Imberbus event. This amazing spectacle is when roads across Salisbury Plain that are closed for most the year are open for the exclusive operation of many London buses.

On the right, C94 was photographed before the Second World War, when it was operating out of Enfield garage.

When the London Passenger Transport Board was formed on 1 July 1933, it acquired powers to take over all public passenger road services operated within its Special Area. In most cases, this involved the actual purchase of operators, and often included all of their vehicles. The result was a collection of buses and coaches of all shapes, sizes, manufacturers and models, which was not favourable for efficient maintenance.

Quite a few of the smaller operators ran small buses, and to enable some form of standardisation, the Board bought a replacement fleet of Leyland Cub buses with a low seating capacity, which could be used for one-person operation, as allowed within the regulations of the time. Seating was restricted to 20.

The Cubs were for use in both the Central and Country Bus areas and C94 was among the last of the type to be delivered in June 1936. It was allocated initially to Enfield garage for route 205 to Chingford. In 1950 it was repainted green and sent to Hitchin and subsequently to Northfleet.

It was sold out of stock in 1954, rediscovered on a farm in the 1980s and bought for preservation by Alan Cross. Having passed to the London Transport Museum in 1993, it was further renovated and has been kept at Acton Depot ever since. It has appeared recently at the London Bus Museum on loan and at the annual Imberbus event which sees intensive bus services across Salisbury Plain for just one day each year. With its centre accelerator and right-hand crash gear selector, it can be a challenge to drive, but is highly regarded nevertheless.

T448

Originally in service as Green Line coaches, in the picture above T448 was at Leatherhead Station in early post-war years, demoted to a Country Area bus and on a short working of the 462 route.

A distinguishing feature that wasn't entirely successful – in fact, it was a bit heavy-handed and rather clumsy looking – was the attempt at integrating the bonnet, front nearside wing and front valance into the bodywork.

On the left T448 was undergoing restoration work in the London Bus Museum's workshop. These vehicles were coded 9T9 in London Transport's classification system – the first number referred to the chassis, with new variants given the next available number, the letter was the bus class, and the second number referred to the body, again with new variants given the next available number.

Note how the 9T9s also had the entrance door sliding back into an enclosed pocket. Neither this feature, nor the integrated bonnet and wing assembly was repeated on the subsequent 10T10 version of Green Line coaches.

EMERGENCY EXIT ONLY

These interior views of a 9T9 demonstrate how London Transport was advancing the appearance of its buses and coaches in terms of modernity and style as the 1930s progressed.

The influences of the Art Deco and Moderne movements were clearly in evidence. Previously, you could argue coach interiors had more of an Edwardian drawing room look.

Much of this was thanks to Frank Pick, Chief Executive Officer and Vice Chairman of the London Passenger Transport Board at the time.

Pick had a strong interest in design, particularly how it could be used effectively in public life. He commissioned eye-catching commercial art, graphic design and modern architecture. This all helped to turn London Transport into a highly recognisable and admired brand, both for its road and for its Underground services.

What grew into the Green Line coach network began in 1929, when London General started an express service between Watford, Golders Green (for connections with the Underground) and Central London. This was to combat initiatives then being taken by several independent operators around the fringes of London. The network grew rapidly and was formed into Green Line Coaches Ltd in 1930, for which a large batch of AEC Regal single-deck coaches was put into service. By the mid-1930s the need to replace earlier coaches with more comfortable, modern types led to the purchse of 50 up-to-date Regals with stylish bodies built by Weymann at Addlestone and delivered in 1936. T448 was initially allocated to Hitchin garage for routes K1/K2 between Dorking/Horsham and Baldock/Hitchin.

Anticipating reduced fuel and rubber supplies reaching the UK with the advent of war in 1939, Green Line coach services were withdrawn. T448, along with many other Green Line coaches, was converted into an ambulance to help with the evacuation of patients from central London hospitals at high risk from bombing.

In 1946 it was reconverted for normal passenger use but, as these 9T9s were rather underpowered for rigorous Green Line schedules, it became a Country Area bus. In 1953 it was sold to Harperbury Hospital near St Albans. After its engine failed, it was left to rot in the undergrowth until recognised and rescued for preservation in 1968 on behalf of the London Bus Preservation Trust and becoming part of the London Bus Museum collection.

260

In the picture above, 260 was coming along Craven Park on its way into Harlesden and ultimately Hammersmith. Willesden Power Station can be seen in the background. Built in 1903, this was coal-fired until 1972 and subsequently demolished, although not before parts of Ridley Scott's film *Alien* were filmed there. A new Taylors Lane open cycle gas turbine power station was built in 1979.

The trolleybus in front of 260 was 216, another C2-class example, but note the half-spats over the rear wheels.

On the left, 260 in preservation was performing its duties at the East Anglia Transport Museum at Carlton Colville in May 2012.

Again on the 660 route, trolleybus 260 was passing Harlesden's Jubilee Clock, (just poking out above the roof of 260) in the shot on the right. The clock was built in 1888 to commemorate Queen Victoria's Golden Jubilee of the previous year.

London Transport built on the success of London United Tramways' tram-to-trolleybus conversions by continuing this policy from 1933. Following trials with some prototypes of differing configurations, wholesale orders were placed for what was to become London's standard 6-wheel, 70-seat trolleybus design. The fleet eventually comprised over 1,800 vehicles at its maximum in 1953.

No. 260 was delivered in July 1936 and allocated to Stonebridge depot, primarily for routes 660 (North Finchley - Hammersmith) and 662 (Paddington Green - Sudbury). It spent its entire 23-year life at this depot before being withdrawn in August 1959, having been earmarked for preservation at Clapham's Museum of British Transport. At the last minute, trolley 1253 was substituted (now in the London Transport Museum collection) and 260 was sold to Cohen's, the scrap dealers who broke up most of London's trolleys.

260 was bought by Fred Ivey in a remarkable leap of faith, given that there was nowhere to operate it on a regular basis. It went to Reading for a tour of that system in 1967 and to Bournemouth in 1968. Eventually it was moved to the East Anglia Transport Museum at Carlton Colville near Lowestoft.

Bhs

The shop nearest us on the right in this picture was British Home Stores, a British department store chain founded in 1928 that was best known for selling household items and clothing, and really was a stalwart of the British High Street.

In later years, it embraced furniture, electronics, entertainment, convenience groceries and beauty products. In many ways it was a rival to Woolworths and the stores had a not dissimilar decor.

At the time it folded in late August 2016, by then known as just BHS, there were 163 stores throughout the UK and 74 abroad.

Trolleybus route 662 ran between
Paddington and Sudbury more or less straight along the Harrow Road.
Here, trolleybus 260 was on its way westwards towards Sudbury.

"Drinka Pinta Milka Day" on the poster on the right was the slogan coined by
Bertrand Whitehead for the national Milk Marketing Board's advertising campaign
which first appeared in 1958 and ran for several years. The campaign was introduced
to counter the drop in milk sales following price increases after withdrawal of
government subsidies to milk producers in 1956. It appeared on
the sides of buses, too. The slogan was still
in use in the 1970s.

On the right in this picture is the Metropolitan Electric Tramways war memorial at Stonebridge trolleybus depot. After the depot closed the memorial was repositioned in Barham Park, Sudbury, as the official war memorial of the London Borough of Brent.

C111

C111 was heading a line-up at Epsom Racecourse on Derby Day, 5 June 1948, in the picture below. Behind it was an STL and, behind that, one of the rear-engined Cubs featured on pages 70-71.

The two colour pictures on the opposite page show C111 resplendent at the night-time launch after its 2022 restoration.

An interesting service provided by London Transport was the Inter Station route connecting the principal London main line termini for the benefit of railway passengers who needed to transfer across London when making through journeys. Initially, it operated throughout the day but later was restricted to evenings and through the night. Ample luggage capacity was required and to that end special half-deck bodies were built on a small batch of Leyland Cubs in 1936. The raised seating area towards the rear of the vehicles enabled a capacious luggage boot to be fitted underneath. Later in their careers, working agreements with various airlines meant that some of these Cubs were used for airport services and sometimes sign-written for the airlines for which they worked.

C111 was worked mainly by Old Kent Road garage but spent some time during the Second World War allocated to ENSA (Entertainments National Service Association) to assist with the transport of entertainers and their props between engagements.

It was sold in 1953 to the London Fire Brigade for use as a personnel carrier, but was bought for private preservation in 1961. A major restoration was completed in 2022, and the vehicle relaunched in early May 2022 at a night-time photoshoot that took in a number of London railway termini.

With reference to the Inter Station Cubs being used by airlines, in this picture on the left C106 was on hire to BEA around 1951, still with the Railway Air Services name on the side.

Railway Air Services was formed in March 1934 by the big four railway companies and Imperial Airways. It was a domestic airline with routes within the United Kingdom to link up with Imperial's overseas flights.

When the UK government formed BOAC and BEA in 1946, BEA was given a monopoly of scheduled air services within the United Kingdom and to continental Europe. So, from 1 August that year, Railway Air Services operated all its services on behalf of BEA until it ceased operations on 31 January 1947. Aircraft, staff and routes all then passed to BEA.

The vehicles used
by Hearn were not acquired
by London Transport for the
reasons explained in
this memo.

LONDON TRANSPORT.

DEPARTMENT OF THE CHIEF ENGINEER - BUSES AND COACHES.

OFFICE OF THE TECHNICAL OFFICER.

INTER-STATION BUS SERVICE.

In connection with the **proposed** acquisition of the above
services by the Board an inspection has been made of the vehicles
at present engaged on this work and being operated by Mr. P. Hearn,
a list of these vehicles being given below:-

TYPE.	RGSTED: NO.	PLATE NO.	SEATING.	CERT:OF FITNESS EXPIRED.	H.P.	YEAR AND DATE OF MANFTR:	REMARKS.	
Daimler.	XL.9896	2315N	14	29.11.37.	27	9. 9.23.	Condition good.	X
"	XV.3094	1506N	"	8. 1.36.	"	31.10.28.	-Do-	
"	YH.1360	1507N	"	31. 1.38.	"	17. 5.27.	"	X
"	YW.6758	1938N	"	30. 4.36.	"	11. 6.28.	"	
"	WR.2718	1503N	"	31. 1.38.	"	15. 1.21.	"	Y
"	YW.7596	1958N	"	17. 5.36.	"	15. 6.28.	"	
"	YW. 772	1173N	12	28.12.35.		11. 5.28.		

X = Single rear tyres.

It will be seen from the above that on a ten years' life basis
none of the vehicles have more than **three years'** remaining life, and
that in two cases the vehicles have already been in service between
12 and 14 years. It was noticeable that the buses had been extremely
well maintained and were in excellent condition, although of obsolete
design both in respect of the bodies and the chassis.

The Daimler type of engine has been found **very** unsatisfactory
owing to a tendency for excessive lubricating oil consumption, and
difficulties of maintenance connected with the operation of the sleeve valves.

The bodies illustrated in the photographs appended to this
report are of obsolete design, and, in most cases, the headroom is
extremely low.

Whilst, therefore, the vehicles are at the present moment
in an extremely good condition, it is considered that to operate these
buses under the Board's conditions will present difficulty from the
maintenance aspect. Furthermore, owing to the obsolete design, it
will undoubtedly be necessary for them to be replaced very shortly.

In view of the age of the vehicles concerned, and their
obsolete design, it is considered inadvisable for the Board to purchase
these buses for operation on the Inter-Station services, and it is
recommended that after due consideration by the Operating Department
in regard to the optimum seating capacity for this work a special type
of vehicle should be designed using one of our existing standard types
of chassis.

It is estimated that provided authority be given prior to
December 1st, 1935, it will be possible to have the required number
of vehicles available for service by July 1st, 1936, and that arrangements
should, therefore, be made with Mr. Hearn for the existing vehicles to
be operated by him for a period of six months, dating from January 1st,
1936.

H.1/GH.
20. 9. 1935.

TECHNICAL OFFICER.

In October 1936 the London Passenger Transport Board acquired an existing inter-station service, which had been started by 'Patsy' Hearn in July 1928, sponsored by some of the main-line railway companies. The new route ran between Victoria and King's Cross Stations via Paddington, Marylebone, Euston and St Pancras on Mondays to Saturdays only. From April 1937 the route also served Waterloo Station, and shortly thereafter a Sunday service began. The service was never given a route number; it ran during the day and evening (but not at night) until September 1939, when it was withdrawn following the outbreak of the Second World War. At the request of the Minister of War Transport the service was reinstated from 20 December 1943, with daily evening journeys and a limited night service.

During the period the service was not running, some (maybe all) of the Inter Station Cubs had been made available to ENSA (Entertainments National Service Association). Four had been returned to work the Inter Station service following reinstatement in late 1943, but the full evening service required five buses and double-deck ST613 was repainted into the blue Inter Station livery to be the fifth.

From April 1944 the service became a circular route from Waterloo, operating daily in both directions via Victoria, Paddington, Euston and King's Cross. The service now ran every 30 minutes from 6pm until about midnight, requiring five buses, with one bus remaining in service for a limited night service.

From 2 May 1945 the vehicle allocation became five STs – maybe the Cub seating capacity of 20 was now too small for the number of passengers the service was carrying? The STs seated 40, with some seats removed for extra luggage space. It should be remembered that during the Second World War and for some years thereafter, serving soldiers, sailors and airmen carrying their bulky kitbags, and often unfamiliar with London's geography, made up a good proportion of the passengers carried. But the Cubs continued to be used from time to time, the last use being recorded in November 1950.

From November 1950 the service changed again. The evening journeys were withdrawn and the service now became all-night only, every night, and mostly running Waterloo - Victoria - Paddington - Euston - King's Cross - Waterloo. Route allocation was now RTs in standard red livery with no special provision for extra luggage, seating 56; extra luggage was placed on spare seats. Routemaster buses replaced the RTs by early 1964.

From September 1964 the Inter Station service became irregular, operated on Sunday night/Monday mornings only, supplemented in summer by journeys on Friday and Saturday nights.

It was revitalised from 16 May 1980, with hourly departures on Friday, Saturday and Sunday nights on a circular Waterloo - Victoria - Paddington - Euston - St Pancras - King's Cross - St Pancras - Euston - Waterloo route. The Friday night service ended in September 1980, but the Saturday and Sunday night operations continued. By now the allocation was one MD-class Metro-Scania Metropolitan bus, changed in early 1981 to a DM-class Daimler Fleetline, and changing again in November 1983 to one T-class Leyland Titan.

The route operated for the last time on 21/22 April 1985. It was absorbed into new routes N50/N51, which were fully integrated into London's night bus services. They stopped at all bus stops – the Inter Station route had run non-stop between the main-line stations, and since the introduction of the route it had always had a flat-fare. Initially the adult fare was one shilling and this had been increased to one pound by the time the route was discontinued.

STL 2093

Having decided to standardise on the 56-seat diesel-powered open platform, crew-operated double-decker with pre-selector gearbox for the majority of the busier routes, London Transport had many hundreds built through the 1930s, 1940s and 1950s.

The link with AEC ensured that the Southall factory continued to supply the Regent chassis in STL form with most of the bodies built by London Transport itself at Chiswick. However, STL 2093 was delivered in 1937 with a Park Royal steel-framed body. The bus operated from Cricklewood garage on the busy Edgware Road trunk routes, but was damaged in an air-raid during the Second World War and sent to Birmingham Corporation Transport for repair.

The Park Royal bodies were not very durable and developed a sag along the waistline. STL 2093's was replaced in 1949 by a Chiswick built body transferred from another member of the class.

It was withdrawn from service in 1955 and went on to work for Reliance Motor Services of Newbury in Berkshire. It was one of a small number of STLs sold for further service; most were scrapped as being beyond economical repair following service through the war years and beyond, long after they should have been retired.

It was bought for preservation in 1958, an early example of private acquisition, and went through several owners before being acquired by the London Bus Preservation Trust. Although restoration work had been carried out over the years, it needs further extensive attention.

The current condition of STL 2093 has allowed the London Bus Museum to display it in the War Hall at the Museum to demonstrate a damaged wartime bus. In the picture above the bus was in the Museum before the War Hall was constructed around the bus.

It has masked headlamps and other wartime requirements and is shown in the state in which many preserved buses arrive in the restorers' workshops, with panels removed to show the part-timber construction of the body.

Eccleston Bridge, near Victoria Station, used to be a hub for Green Line, with many Green Line routes passing through.

Occasionally, ordinary buses would substitute for Green Line coaches and, in the picture above, red-liveried STL2093 was on a relief working of Green Line route 703 to Wrotham while on loan to Swanley garage in June 1949, shortly after receiving its replacement body.

On the left STL2093 was in Whitehall on route 77 heading for Tooting on 19 April 1952.

STL 2377

Although clearly not anywhere between Sloane Square and Festival Gardens, nevertheless this beautiful shot with passengers in the clothes of the day perfectly evokes the early post-war years of an STL.

This STL is a remarkable example of bus restorers' skills. The bus was withdrawn by London Transport in 1954 and then run by Jack Mulley of Ixworth in Suffolk on contract duties to local factories until 1961. Like most of Jack's second-line buses and coaches it was taken out of service and stored before being bought for preservation in 1966. Some restoration was carried out then but it was never fully completed. The bus joined the London Bus Preservation Trust in 1994 and a complete restoration started. This was hugely expensive, but greatly helped by generous assistance from the Science Museum Prism Fund, the bus having been recognised as a significant example of the pre-war London motorbus. The work was finished in 2000, complete with period advertisements, and the result was highly reminiscent of the comprehensive overhauls which London Transport applied to its fleet at Chiswick and Aldenham Works.

STL2377 is a standard AEC Regent with body built by London Transport itself. It features a pre-selector gearbox, with the speed change lever mounted on the floor and looking like a standard gear lever to the uninitiated. Gears are selected ahead of their need by positioning this lever and the actual change made by depressing and then releasing the operating pedal. This is in the same position as a clutch pedal but the speed change method thus adopted means that the driver can use both hands on the steering wheel while changing gear with his left foot. This is particularly useful when negotiating traffic hazards such as right and left turns. This transmission system was specified right through to the end of the 1950s for the RT/ RTL/RTW/RLH/RF London bus family and was eventually superseded by the semi- or fully automatic device fitted to Routemasters.

Presented in superb condition by the London Bus Museum, with an immaculate blind display, STL2377 was proceeding towards Watford along Bushey Heath High Road on the Watford Running Day on 30 March 2014 in the picture below.

In the view above STL2377 was passing a Dolcis shoe shop in Barking on 27 November 1951.

Dolcis started as a street barrow in 1863 when John Upson began to sell his shoes at Woolwich Town Market. His first store was in Woolwich, named the Great Boot Provider. The company went public in 1920 and the name Dolcis appeared.

STL2377 was in Mulley's Motorways livery at Ixworth sometime between 1954 and 1961 in the picture below. It was bought for preservation in that latter year and the photograph may well have been taken on the day it was collected.

T504

F urther Green Line coaches were added to the fleet in 1938. These were a development of the previous design on AEC Regal chassis, the 9T9s, and were coded 10T10. The bodies were built at Chiswick and are generally regarded as the most elegant and stylish of all the T-class Green Line coaches, and the most successful. Gone was the clumsy integrated bonnet, wing and valance construction of the 9T9s, and the door slid into a recess rather than a pocket. There were other minor differences, internally too. They certainly gave the Green Line network a thoroughly modern, smart image.

There were 266 10T10s in total. T504, delivered in April 1938, first went into service on route D from Staines garage, operating between Staines and Sevenoaks via Kingston, Central London, Bromley and Westerham.

On display at Wisley Airfield before Brooklands became the home for the London Bus Museum's events, T504 was alongside more modern interpretations of the Green Line image designed by Best Impressions.

During its later years as a red bus, T504 was photographed in Kingston on 27 September 1952 in the picture at the top of the opposite page.

On the right you can see the cleaner look to the front end compared with the 9T9 version, and how the door slid back into a recess rather than an enclosed pocket.

Like T448, it was also converted for use as an ambulance in 1939, but after the war was returned to Green Line use in 1946. With the arrival of new RF coaches from 1951 onwards, all pre-war coaches soon disappeared from Green Line work. At its second overhaul in 1951, T504 was repainted red and put to work in the Central Bus area, then sold in July 1954.

It survived two attempts at conversion into a goods vehicle by successive owners, firstly as a mobile showroom and then as a mobile crane. It was bought from a scrapyard in Lancashire by the 2RT2 Group in 1968 and restored to Green Line livery. It joined the London Bus Preservation Trust fleet in 1976 and in 1983 it was the subject of a partial restoration by London Transport apprentices at Aldenham Works.

RT 1

By 1937/38 London Transport engineers' thoughts were turning to the design of a successor to the ST/STL classes. The usual collaboration with AEC resulted in an updated Regent chassis powered by a 100bhp engine driving through an air-operated pre-selector gearbox with the control lever on the side of the steering column rather than floor-mounted, as on previous designs. Braking was an air-assisted system instead of vacuum. The new chassis had an obsolete body from an older bus and was tested in this disguised form.

The body of RT1 was designed and built at Chiswick and in 1939 mounted onto the trial chassis. It was of a very stylish, modern appearance and destined to become a classic design which, many would agree, outstripped contemporary offerings from other builders. It entered service from Putney (Chelverton Road) garage and was soon joined by 150 others through to 1942. The designation 'pre-war RT' has been applied by many to these buses but, strictly speaking, only RT1 fits that description, with the others being delivered after rather than before the outbreak of war on 3 September 1939. RT1 was the precursor of over 7,000 similar vehicles which formed the massive fleet replacing pre-war motorbuses, trams and trolleybuses. It was designed to fit London Transport's impressive overhaul systems whereby most mechanical units were interchangeable between vehicles, as were bodies.

RT1's body, however, has an interesting story. It was placed onto another RT chassis as RT19 in 1945 and the original chassis broken up. A further change took place in 1954, when a post-war AEC Regent chassis from RT1420 (whose body had suffered low bridge damage) was used and the bus converted into a Mobile Instruction Unit as 1037J in London Transport's service vehicle fleet. It appears to have been little used in this role and spent many years in a semi-derelict state inside West Ham garage. In 1979 the vehicle was bought by Prince Marshall, restored for passenger use, and certified for public commercial operation displaying its original registration number. Following Prince's premature death in 1981, the bus was sold to Bevan Funnel Ltd and exported to the USA.

Surrounded by wartime utility buses, RT19, carrying its original RT1 body, was outside Morden Station on 17 February 1950 in the picture below.

On the London Bus Museum's route 65 running day on 11 April 2021, RT1 in its original, more ornate livery was heading southwards towards Hook.

Having been recognised as an important survivor of the classic London bus design of the 1940s/50s, it was repatriated in 1986 and a serious and expensive restoration was begun while it was in private ownership. The owner had a desire to sell the bus but wanted it to remain in the UK if sufficient funds could be raised to recoup some of the money he had paid out.

A funding appeal was launched in 2009 by the London Bus Preservation Trust and the bus saved for posterity. Further work has resulted in the body having the appearance of the vehicle as it was first built with a silver roof.

CR16

The little Leyland Cub REC was an ill-fated foray by London Transport and Leyland Motors engineers into alternative positions for engine, gearbox and transmission on passenger vehicles. The major components were all mounted at the rear of the bus in line with the chassis rather than transversely, as was done in later years on the Leyland Atlantean and Daimler Fleetline of the late 1950s onwards.

The bus was intended as an alternative to the conventional C-type for one-person operation on less busy routes. However, mechanical unreliability and little and falling demand for small buses led to many of the class of 49 vehicles becoming redundant. A brief resurrection saw many being used as relief buses during the Olympic Games in London in 1948, but by 1953 all of the class had been withdrawn and sold to dealers, particularly North's in Leeds and Vass at Ampthill in Bedfordshire.

Many of the CR class were exported to Cyprus, including CR16. This bus was repatriated in 1979 in a poor state and rebuilt under the auspices of the then owner, Malcolm Skevington, using parts from CR36. Having been on loan to the London Bus Museum since 2011, it was acquired by the museum in 2017 and at the time of writing is on public display in the green Country Area livery in which it briefly operated from East Grinstead garage in 1948/49 on the very rural 494. This route was introduced after the Second World War and ran up through Lingfield, Crowhurst and Tandridge to Oxted a few times a day.

The two colour pictures show CR16 recreating the 387 route between Tring and the village of Aldbury in August 2010.

LONDON TRANSPORT

FXT122

On the left, CR16 was working a Central Area relief duty of the 133, still showing its wartime white-painted front corners.

At the bottom of this page CR16 in green livery had broken down in Malden Road, Worcester Park sometime in 1948.

RT 113

Following the launch of RT1 after exhaustive testing, London Transport ordered 150 RT types to a basically similar specification. Differences were that RT1's body was partly metal framed, with a cantilevered staircase and platform as on post-war RTs – the first 150 production RTs are wooden-framed, with the rear end supported by a chassis extension. These 150 production RTs are the so-called 'pre-war RTs' which were in fact delivered after the outbreak of the Second World War in 1939. The official type code was 2RT2. Just 10 buses had been delivered by the last day of 1939, with the remaining 140 being available by the end of 1942.

However, they got off to a difficult start because of serious mechanical issues. The compressors delivering air to the braking system were quickly found to be erratic in operation, leading to buses being taken off the road while a cure was found and modifications made. There were delays because of the difficulties in getting parts as Britain geared up for the war effort and also because of air raids. At one stage in August 1940 only 20 buses were licensed from a total of 108 then delivered; the rest were in store. This contributed to the need to seek loans of buses from operators all over the country to help London Transport in its hour of need.

By 1955 all London Transport's pre-war buses had been retired and deliveries of the post-war RT family had been completed. It was logical, therefore, that the 2RT2s should go next. Many became driver training buses or were used to transport staff to and from the overhaul works at Aldenham in Hertfordshire (misnamed, because the works were actually close to Elstree village and Aldenham was a good three miles away!).

Seven were painted into green livery to allow route 327 to continue with double-deck buses until a weak bridge at Broxbourne had been replaced (the 2RT2 was lighter than the post-war RT) but these, the last of the type in passenger service, were withdrawn in September 1957. All 2RT2s had been sold by March 1964.

Apart from RT1 (on RT1420's chassis), four other complete 2RT2 buses remain in existence – RT 8, 44, 54 and 113. RT113 had been new in March 1940 and was bought by a pioneering group of enthusiasts in May 1963 following detailed inspection of all the available 2RT2s as they came up for sale by London Transport.

After a long period of frustrating searches for suitable storage facilities, and of sourcing parts and repairing sections of the vehicle, it is pleasing to note that RT113 remains in the ownership of the 2RT2 Preservation Group, albeit with inevitable changes to the Group's composition, nearly 60 years after sale by London Transport.

The picture at the top of the opposite page was taken outside the RAF Museum at Hendon in 2010 on the occasion of the 70th anniversary commemoration of the Battle of Britain, with three of the original RT-type buses which have been preserved – RT1, RT8 and RT113.

These buses had entered service in London by June 1940, before the Battle of Britain began, so their participation in the 2010 commemoration was appropriate. The white edging on the front mudguards of RT8 and RT113 was added to buses during the Second World War to make them more visible during the blackout.

Above, RT113 was in a Surrey lane on a spring day in April 2006 on a passenger-carrying journey during a bus rally held at the old site of the London Bus Museum in Redhill Road, Cobham.

In the black and white picture to the left, RT113 was on route 30 between Hackney Wick and Roehampton on 4 October 1954.

STL 2674

one that got away

As noted in this book, T31 was the first London bus to be privately preserved by enthusiasts in 1956, and £45 (equivalent to around £1,200 in 2022) was paid for the single-decker. But there was an earlier, unsuccessful, private attempt to acquire, and preserve, a London bus. This was in 1954, and concerned double-deck STL2674. The potential buyers called themselves the STL2674 Purchasing Committee and Alan Cross acted as Secretary. The offer by London Transport to the Purchasing Committee was to sell them the bus for £110, plus £35 for the tyres (equivalent to perhaps £4,000 in 2022). The bus was to be collected from Chiswick Works and London Transport would supply batteries and fuel to get the bus (on trade plates – it was not taxed) to the location where the purchasers would store it. London Transport required that the bus would not be used to carry fare-paying passengers at any time, or for any use where a profit could be made.

The photograph here shows STL2674 at Hackney Garage in August 1954 when it was in use as a staff bus. It had been taken into stock by London Transport in February 1942, and had an AEC chassis of the type commonly referred to as 'unfrozen', meaning it was constructed from parts in existence when the Second World War broke out in 1939, but had not previously been built up to a chassis – the parts had been, by Ministry order, 'frozen' at that time, until the rules were relaxed in 1941. The body placed on STL2674's chassis was not a new build but, unusually, a very early STL body built at London General's Chiswick Works in 1933, with 60 seats in a rather boxy shape, sometimes called Bluebird style. It was this that made the potential acquisition of this bus of some interest. Although originally in red livery, the bus spent its passenger-carrying life in the Country Area, and from 1944 was painted in green livery. It was still in green when the possible sale in 1954 was contemplated.

But the sale did not take place. There was difficulty in raising the required cash and, even if that had been achieved, as many private purchasers of a bus have since discovered, buying is the easy part. Significant and continuing expenditure is then required on maintenance, restoration and storage. But it's a pity the bus was not saved. Few enough of the STL type (London's standard double-deck bus of the 1930s) have survived, and none with the 60-seat Bluebird style of body.

In the picture below, STL2674 in green Country Area livery was on the 362 route between Chesham, Amersham and High Wycombe in early post-war years. It was passing Amersham bus garage with a 10T10 Green Line coach (see pages 66-67) for the 709 to Uxbridge, London, Croydon and Godstone beyond the bus stop shelter.

Haliborange was being advertised on the side of STL2674. Haliborange was marketed as the "nicest way of taking halibut liver oil". It appeared in the 1930s when children were increasingly being given fish oil supplements to provide vitamins A, C and D, and the company boasted about its fresh juicy orange flavour and that the syrup had no fishy taste.

Under the Welfare Food Scheme introduced in the Second World War, fish oil liquid was distributed free to pregnant and nursing mothers and to children up to five years old.

Haliborange produced its first compressed tablet containing vitamins A, C and D in the 1950s, an early chewable flavoured tablet aimed at encouraging children to take their daily vitamin pill.

London's route numbers

I n Victorian times horse-buses did not carry route numbers. They were painted in different liveries for different routes, with boards fixed on the outside showing the locations served. The Vanguard company in 1906 first introduced route numbers on its motorbuses, which were all painted in a red livery, and these route numbers allowed the same bus to work on different routes by just changing the route number and the destination boards. London's largest bus company, London General, acquired Vanguard in 1908 and adopted its red livery and route numbers for all its motorbus services. London General issued its first bus map in 1911, titled Open Air to Everywhere, which showed 23 numbered motorbus services. The lowest numbered was route 1 (Tower Bridge Road - Dollis Hill) and the highest 33 (Oxford Circus - Zoological Gardens, the latter better known today as London Zoo in Regent's Park).

Traces of some of those earliest numbered bus routes can still be found today. Route 9 in the 1911 map between Liverpool Street and Barnes can be traced in today's route 9 between Aldwych and Hammersmith, and route 11 between Liverpool Street and Shepherd's Bush to today's route 11 between Liverpool Street and Fulham. It was in December of the next year, 1912, that the first suffix-letter route was introduced when route 35A began running between Walthamstow and Elephant & Castle. Suffix letters to indicate variants from the main route became very common thereafter until the 77A, the last suffix-lettered route, running between Aldwych and Wandsworth, was renumbered to 87 in 2006.

The London Traffic Act of 1924 was the first piece of legislation to regulate bus services in London. Prior to that date the Metropolitan Police licensed vehicles (buses, taxis and trams) under the Metropolitan Public Carriage Act of 1869, but once the licence was granted the holder had complete freedom to operate as desired. By the early 1920s the view was that bus services should now be licensed, not least to eliminate wasteful competition and manage increasing traffic congestion. The Metropolitan Police, through its Traffic Division, took on this new responsibility.

The head of the Traffic Division was Arthur Ernest Bassom OBE KPM, a remarkable man. Born in 1865, he had first joined the Royal Marine Artillery, but in 1886 left to join the Metropolitan Police as a Constable. He quickly transferred to the Public Carriage Office and rose through the ranks, becoming Chief Inspector and placed in charge of the Public Carriage Office in 1901. He was promoted to Superintendent in 1906.

This was when motor vehicles were taking over from horse-drawn vehicles and, faced with the new motor taxis, Bassom devised the Conditions of Fitness for taxis in 1906. Since then, these have formed some of the design requirements for London taxis, such as the requirement for a 25-foot turning circle. When the Traffic Division was created in 1921, Bassom was appointed to head it up, with the rank of Chief Superintendent. His reputation was that of a workaholic with a very detailed knowledge of London's streets and traffic conditions, and of the construction and engineering characteristics of motor taxis and buses. Due to retire in 1925 at the age of 60, he was happy to continue in office and was promoted in that year to Chief Constable, Director of Traffic Services.

Bassom turned his attention to London bus route numbering, and devised a system since known as the Bassom Scheme, under which suffix letters ran riot. The longest journey on any route was given the basic route number, and short-workings on that route, which did not reach one or either of the ultimate termini, were given a suffix letter. The problem was that, on many routes, the ultimate terminus was only reached infrequently, so almost all buses on that route would display a suffix letter.

To take the example of route 11, although this usually ran between Liverpool Street and Shepherd's Bush, while the British Empire Exhibition of 1924/1925 was on at Wembley, the route was extended to the Exhibition Grounds. So under Bassom, route 11 was shown only on buses running between Liverpool Street and Wembley. Those buses operating on the route over a shorter distance showed route 11 with a suffix letter as follows:

11A Aldwych – Shepherd's Bush

11B Liverpool Street – Victoria

11C Aldwych – Hammersmith

11D Liverpool Street – Hammersmith

11E Shepherd's Bush – Walham Green (later Liverpool Street – Shepherd's Bush)

11F Victoria – Hammersmith

Bassom died in 1926, but his numbering scheme lived on. It was not until 1934 that buses on the principal route 11 between Liverpool Street and Shepherd's Bush were renumbered from 11E to 11, with no suffix letter. At the same time as dropping the Bassom suffix letters, the new London Passenger Transport Board introduced a new route numbering scheme under which blocks of numbers were reserved for different services, as follows:

1–199 Central Area (red) double-deck routes

200–289 Central Area single-deck routes

290–299 Central Area night routes

300–399 Country Area (North) (green) routes

400–499 Country Area (South) (green) routes

Suffix letters were now not used for short-workings, but as before, were used for variations from the principal route. Tram routes were not renumbered and remained in a separate 1-99 series, and as more trolleybus routes were introduced, they were numbered in a 500-699 series.

Green Line routes used letters before they were withdrawn at the start of the Second World War, but when services were reintroduced in the post-war period, they were numbered in the 700-799 series.

New sequences started in the 1950s with the growth in Country Area bus services, and numbers in the 800-849 series were introduced in the Country Area (North) with 850 and upwards in the Country Area (South). Finally, and much later, routes were numbered in the 900-series for Mobility Bus services and in the 600-series for school bus services. This system broadly remained intact for many years, but the rigid separation in the Central Area between double-deck and single-deck routes broke down from the 1940s onwards.

In 1960 the night bus routes were renumbered with an N prefix instead of a separate 2XX series, and when the Red Arrow services were introduced in 1966 they were given numbers in the 500 series, all trolleybuses having been withdrawn by then, leaving the numbers vacant. From 1968 onwards the shortening in length of many bus routes led to a need for more route numbers. Local flat-fare services used a system of letter prefixes in order to distinguish them from traditional services with graduated fares. In due course all bus fares were made the same and the need for the distinction was lost, although many letter-prefixed routes remain.

Meanwhile, after 1970 when the Country Area network of London Transport was transferred to London Country Bus Services, the old series of 300-499 numbers for routes in the Home Counties began to break down. Many new routes in what has become the Transport for London (TfL) area are now numbered in the 300s and 400s.

G 351

The need to divert manufacturing resources and materials to essential and mainly military uses during the years of the Second World War meant severely curtailing the production of non-essential items. Manufacture, strictly controlled by the Ministry of Supply, was to utility standards that reduced the need for skilled labour and kept frills to an absolute minimum. Manufacture of double-deck bus chassis was limited to Guy, Bristol and Daimler, and single-deckers to Bedford; and only a small number of body builders for both types.

Allocation of new vehicles was on the basis of need being demonstrated for transport of war workers, where civilian transport would be severely disrupted and where operators had lost vehicles to enemy action. London Transport had 181 motorbuses completely destroyed (plus 17 trolleybuses and 77 trams) and many others severely damaged. Then there were those beyond repair, or for which parts weren't available, and those lost or damaged through accidents in the blackout.

London Transport was allocated 756 utility buses, all double-deckers. These began to be delivered from 1941, but some didn't arrive until after the war ended, including G351, which arrived in January 1946. They were to very basic standards with angular bodywork (to avoid skilled metal-working), wooden slatted seats and single-skinned panelling which encouraged condensation. They had crash gearboxes at a time when London Transport's drivers were used to the more refined pre-select gearchange methods.

Their basic construction and non-standard specification meant these stop-gap deliveries would be disposed of as soon as delivery of post-war buses permitted. Thus, most had gone to dealers by the end of 1953. Given that other operators up and down the country, and abroad, were desperate for replacement buses, and that the London Transport utilities were mostly less than 10 years old, many found new homes. Burton-upon-Trent Corporation bought some of the Guys, but these, too, were sold for scrap as soon as newer buses were available.

A self-confessed Guy enthusiast, Rev. John Lines MBE bought G351 from Burton in 1967, still with its original wartime body. As was the case with many of the early bus preservationists, John experienced challenges with cash flow for restoration, repairs and storage. It's good that he persisted because G351 is the only remaining London utility bus. He donated it to the London Bus Preservation Trust in 1980 and the bus has subsequently been rebuilt with the valuable assistance of the Science Museum Prism Fund.

Looking resplendent in its preserved condition, G351 was in Parliament Square in July 2013 on the opposite page and, above, in Horse Guards Avenue in April 2016.

G351 was turning right from High Street into South Street by the Golden Lion in Romford in July 1951.

RT 2657

After the Second World War London Transport embarked on a massive programme to replace time-expired and utility motorbuses and to close the tramway network.

The work undertaken pre-war on the AEC Regent RT was considered to be a satisfactory basis for a standardised double-deck fleet. The concept of standardisation included the interchangeability of bodies and chassis between vehicles which would fit its 'factory line' bus overhaul system. The new works at Aldenham, recently released from wartime aircraft parts manufacture and assembly, would be used, primarily for body overhauls.

RT2657 was allocated to Peckham garage (code PM) between April 1962 and July 1964. On the left at the top it was at Shoreditch Church on a foggy day, all steamed up inside and with the lights on, awaiting a turn on the 78 over Tower Bridge and down to Peckham and Dulwich. The 78 once went further south to West Wickham.

On the left, RT2657 was on display at a London Bus Museum Spring Gathering.

In the big picture, RT2657 was passing The Greyhound at the bottom of Peckham Hill Street at the junction with Peckham High Road. This time the bus was on the 63 from King's Cross.

Ultimately, over 7,000 new double-deck buses would be delivered between 1947 and 1954. The majority were on the Regent chassis, but subsequent contractual and supply issues led to over 2,100 chassis orders going to Leyland Motors.

Contracts for body construction were placed with Park Royal Vehicles, Weymann and Saunders. A small batch of RTs was bodied by Cravens of Sheffield (see the section on RT1431).

RT2657 has an interesting history. London Transport's overhaul system meant that the fleet number, or 'bonnet' number as it was sometimes called, was just that: a number teamed with a conventional registration number. Every chassis and body also had their own numbers and a mix and match process meant that a bus with, for example, fleet number RT2657, went into the works with a particular chassis and body combination but came out, usually, with a different combination. This method was approved by the Ministry of Transport and saved time and road tax. The chassis of RT2657 started life as RT501 and the body as RT677 but went through several changes at each overhaul.

RT2657 was withdrawn from service in 1964 and was acquired by the Paris Transport Museum. However, it rarely ventured outside and was offered to the London Bus Museum in 2012 for a nominal sum of one euro.

T792

Above, preserved T792 was performing on a Hemel Hempstead Running Day at Watford Junction in June 2008, in company with a green Country Area liveried Cravens bodied RT, RT1499.

On the right, T792 was in its operational days at Uxbridge Bus Station, working route 309 from Watford Leavesden Road garage (WT).

T792 was allocated to WT from new in July 1948 until the garage closed in 1952 and then it was transferred to the new garage at Garston (GR).

On the opposite page, T792 was at Chorleywood Station on a running day in 2012.

The final batch of front-engined, single-deck buses was 30 AEC Regal IIIs for the Country Area, all with bodies built by Mann Egerton similar to TD95 shown on pages 90-91, although with sliding entrance doors. They were classified in London Transport's nomenclature as 15T13 and were the most powerful of all the Ts, entering service in 1948 from Watford Leavesden Road and Hemel Hempstead garages.

Originally in green with white window surrounds, at their first overhaul in 1950-1951 they were repainted all-over green with just a thin line of cream below the windows. Three were sent to the Central Area in 1956 – T785, 794 and 796 – at first operating out of Kingston garage on route 216, but then moved to Norbiton to work the 201. They were never repainted red and later returned to the Country Area.

By the summer of 1958 only five were scheduled for regular service, four at Grays and one at Tring, but Crawley also had one, unofficially, mainly used on the circular 426 route. T787 at Crawley gained fame as being the final 15T13, being delicensed on 13 August 1962, although it was relicensed in October for use as a staff bus until April 1963.

After withdrawal, many of these Ts were sold to the Ceylon Transport Board. A few were sold through dealers to construction contractors in the UK, including T792, the sole remaining example. It went to Bovis at Watford Gap until rescued for preservation in 1971. Having been through several hands it is now in beautiful condition in the ownership of John Herting, who also owns RT2177.

1812

By 1948 London's first trolleybuses, the Diddlers, were overdue for replacement, having worked beyond their intended lifespan due to the Second World War. Their replacements were 77 class Q1 trolleybuses delivered in 1948/49 to Fulwell depot for service on Kingston local routes 601-605. Number 1812 entered service in September 1948. Unlike its buses and coaches, London Transport's trolleybuses never displayed class code prefixes. A further 50 Q1s were delivered in 1952, mainly to replace pre-war trolleybuses at Isleworth and Hanwell depots.

Q1s were handsome looking vehicles and, at 8 feet wide, were extremely comfortable to travel on. LT's original intention had been to keep them until the late 1960s, but negotiations with several trolleybus operators in Spain led to a change of plan, with 125 of the 127 Q1s being withdrawn in 1961 and sold.

The Q1s were replaced in London service by older trolleybuses built in 1938-40 and these, in turn, were replaced by Routemaster buses in May 1962 in the final stage of the Trolleybus Replacement Programme, which involved Fulwell and Isleworth depots.

Trolleybus 1812 had joined the Santander-Astillero fleet in 1961 but, when this system closed down in 1977, it was bought by the British Trolleybus Society and shipped back to the UK. A major restoration project was undertaken, which included reversing the staircase and rear platform layout from the changes made in Spain back to the original UK layout. This was completed in 2001 and the vehicle joined the collection at The Trolleybus Museum at Sandtoft in North Lincolnshire. Following a five-year loan to the London Bus Museum, trolleybus 1812 was overhauled before returning to service at Sandtoft.

Identical vehicle 1768 was kept by the British Transport Commission and is now in the London Transport Museum's Acton Depot for safe storage. Nine London trolleybuses exist in the UK, including examples repatriated after initial disposal for preservation in Paris and in Dublin.

The picture on the left was taken at the Hammersmith trolleybus terminus, at the King Street end of Hammersmith Grove, pedestrianised many years later.

1812 was waiting to leave on the 667 through Brentford and Twickenham to Hampton Court. Behind it was C3-class 329 of 1936 on the 666, which would head up through Acton and Harlesden to Cricklewood and Edgware. In the background to the right of the third trolleybus in view, a 'pre-war' RT was passing by on learner duties.

Below, 1812 was at Shannon Corner, New Malden, on the 605 route, which ran between Teddington, Kingston and Wimbledon.

At the top of this page is 1812 looking quite pristine and running at Sandtoft with red RF366 behind.

This men's tailor and clothing store was founded by Sir Montague Maurice Burton in Chesterfield in 1903 as The Cross-Tailoring Company.

By 1929 it had factories, mills and 400 stores and, when Montague Burton died in 1952, Burton was thought to be the largest multiple tailor in the world.

It became part of the Arcadia Group at the beginning of the 21st century and when that went into administration in 2021, the Burton brand was bought by online retailer Boohoo.com.

Burton was renowned for its Art Deco-inspired store architecture, mostly on corner sites, created by Leeds-based architect Harry Wilson.

RTL139

Despite its favouritism for and close relationship with AEC, London Transport was required to use more than one supplier. So, in the 1950s there were Leyland versions of the RT, based on a modified version of the Leyland Titan PD2 chassis with pre-selector gear changing and air-operated brakes that could take the RT style body. 1,631 RTLs were built that looked similar to the RTs, plus 500 RTWs. The RTWs were London's first 8ft wide double-deck buses (see pages 94-95).

The RTLs were delivered between mid-1948 and autumn 1954, but the last deliveries were stored until spring 1958 before entering service. They had bodywork by Park Royal, Metro-Cammell and Weymann. All were painted red for Central Area use, but in 1960/1961 18 were repainted green for use in the Country Area at Hatfield, but only for 11 months, as they were considered inferior to the AECs by that garage's drivers and engineers. The last RTLs in service ran on 30 November 1968 on routes 176 and 226.

The 500 bodies supplied by Metro-Cammell were not compatible with those built by the other suppliers and had to be interchanged only within their own sub-class, for which the appropriate chassis were modified to accept them.

On the left, RTL139 was outside the original London Bus Museum's site in Redhill Road in Cobham in February 2011.

This bus was allocated to Camberwell garage (code Q) between 1956 and 1960 and on the right it was at Aldgate.

In the shot below, taken in Stratford Broadway in the early 1960s, RTL139 was heading for Aldgate.

RTL139 entered service in March 1949 and was sold out of service in 1967. It was bought by the Nationaal Automobiel Museum near The Hague in the Netherlands, another foreign museum which considered that a London bus was important to its collection. It was repatriated by the LBPT in 1998 and remains internally in almost as-withdrawn condition. It has been used extensively by the London Bus Museum, but has now been withdrawn for mechanical and bodywork attention.

RT 1431

RT1431 was allocated to Uxbridge garage (UX) between March 1953 and September 1954 and in the picture on this page it was photographed in Uxbridge Bus Station on an earlier incarnation of the 220 route number, which was later used for the bus service that replaced the 630 trolleybus route – see pages 138-139.

On the right, in preservation, RT1431 was in Wimbledon on the route 93 running day in 2021. In these pictures you can see the wider upper-deck front and how the Cravens body slightly overhangs the side of the cab.

Even the combined output of RT family bodies from the established bodybuilders of Park Royal, Weymann and Saunders was insufficient for London Transport's needs, so a small batch of 120 was commissioned from Cravens of Sheffield. This firm was well-known both for bus bodies and railway carriages, but could not take on the building of bodies to London Transport's exact specification.

Therefore, the Cravens standard bus body was loosely adapted to look like an RT but was not interchangeable with bodies from the other manufacturers. It kept Cravens' five-bay window layout, and the upper deck front and rear windows were to a different profile from the standard RT body. The sub-type was classified RT3/4 in London Transport's system and the buses were operated in both the Central and Country Bus areas.

Even before the disastrous and prolonged bus crew strike of 1958, which led to many service cuts, it was the case that London Transport's original demand for new buses proved to be significantly in excess of later requirements. As a non-standard type, the Cravens bodied RTs were withdrawn and sold from 1955 and snapped up by operators all over the country keen to buy relatively new vehicles at second-hand prices. One exception was the chassis of Cravens RT1420 which, as already mentioned, is now supporting the original body of RT1 (see pages 68-69).

RT1431 was operated by the A1 Service consortium of Ardrossan in Ayrshire until 1966, when it was bought by yet another keen group of bus enthusiasts, as seen on page 5. It came under the auspices of the fledgling London Omnibus Traction Society; then through several private owners until bought by Ensignbus of Purfleet for its ever-expanding collection of historic buses. Only one other Cravens RT has survived, RT1499 (in green livery), which is also with Ensignbus.

TD 95

Although a new generation of modern, underfloor-engined single-deckers, the RF-class, was to appear at the beginning of the 1950s, London Transport was in dire need of new single-deck buses in the immediate post-war period. It couldn't wait for the RFs, so the Board sanctioned the purchase of more T-class AEC Regals – shown on pages 82-83 – plus 131 similar Leyland Tiger PS1s with manual transmission.

The first 31 Tigers had Weymann bodies with a rather frowning frontal appearance, typical of that body manufacturer, but the second batch of 100 was bodied by the Norwich firm of Mann Egerton, better known for repairing and overhauling existing vehicles than building its own. TD95 from this second batch was delivered to London Transport in May 1949 and allocated to Kingston garage.

TD95 lasted with London Transport until October 1962, its final allocation being Edgware garage. Many TDs were exported for further use in Ceylon (now Sri Lanka) and Yugoslavia. TD95, however, was sold to members of Bromley Technical College at the end of 1963, who, in the summer of 1964, took it to Romania and Hungary and visited Copenhagen, Stockholm, Hamburg, Helsinki, Leningrad, Moscow, Warsaw and Berlin in it. It made further continental journeys successfully and was then sold into preservation in May 1967, arriving at the London Bus Museum's old site at Cobham in 1978. It received a complete restoration in the late 1990s.

Four TD-class Leyland Tigers survive in preservation. There would have been a fifth, but TD121 was vandalised and parts were used in the restoration of TD95.

The Potters Bar to Epping Forest via Waltham Cross 242 route in North East London was operated by TDs between 1949 and 1953, when it went to double-deck operation using RTs.

The picture on the left shows TD95 recreating that era at Northaw against a backdrop of St Thomas à Becket Church, Grade II listed and built in 1881 by C. Kirk and Son of Sleaford.

Route 210 from Golders Green across Hampstead Heath to Highgate and Finsbury Park was for many years operated by single-deckers because of the awkward pinch point at The Spaniards Inn, where the road was squeezed between a tollhouse and the inn.

Once the haunt of highwaymen – Dick Turpin's father was the landlord there – the inn can be traced back to 1585 and the tollhouse to 1710.

When new, TDs worked this route on Sundays only but, by 1949, they were allocated all week.

Recreating those days in the picture above, TD95 was at the westbound stop immediately before the inn.

Route 201 connected Kingston with Hampton Court the indirect way through Surbiton, Long Ditton and Thames Ditton, then continued to Teddington, Hanworth and Feltham Station.

TDs were allocated to the route in 1949 and, on the left, a brand-new TD95 was at Feltham Station with the crew looking on before returning to Kingston.

Two years later the 201 was cut back to run just between Kingston and Hampton Court.

UMP 227

355 RADLETT
TO CAR PARK
UILDERS
CRAFTSMANS
SA17
321
CXX 463
UMP 227

447 WOLDINGHAM
LONDON TRANSPORT
UMP 227

Before AEC launched its
Regal IV model, the company's first post-war
underfloor-engined chassis, it produced prototypes in 1949
in accordance with the regulations of the day. These were 7ft 6in wide and
27ft 6in long and UMP 227 carried a 40-seat body built by Park Royal.

By May 1950, one of these protoypes, having been registered UMP 227, was on
loan to London Transport, who first sent it to St Albans garage, where it was used on
route 355 between Borehamwood, Radlett, St Albans and Harpenden. It then worked
from Reigate garage on the 447 route.

Its performance convinced London Transport that the AEC Regal IV would be its
choice for a new standard single-deck bus and Green Line coach, and it ordered 700
chassis. Technology had moved on from AEC's 1930s dalliance with the side-engined
Q-type and it was now possible to employ a modified standard AEC engine to fit
under the floor of a single-decker, giving the advantage of some commonality of
parts with the front-engined double-deck AEC 9.6 litre engine used for the RT.

After its time with London Transport UMP 227 was demonstrated to several
operators around the country. It returned to AEC at Southall in 1951 for engineers to
experiment on, but the bus was also used for staff transport, still in London Transport
green livery. Somewhat worse for wear, in 1954 it was painted matt grey but by 1959
it was in the AEC/Park Royal service vehicle livery of yellow and blue until bought for
preservation in 1971. Preservation wasn't without its difficulties, but eventually, in
2008, UMP 227 was bought by a consortium of London Bus Museum members and
donated to the Museum. A thorough overhaul and rebuild was completed by 2013.

In the top picture on the opposite page,
UMP 227 was photographed in St Peter's Street
in St Albans, the main stopping point in the
city for buses, during its sojourn at St Albans
garage. It was loading up for the southern part
of its route 355 journey to Radlett.

Subsequently, UMP 227 was sent to Reigate
garage, and was photographed on the 447
terminal stand in Redhill in the lower picture
opposite.

Its regular haunt at Reigate was the 447
route, which performed a local function
around Reigate and Redhill but continued
to Caterham-on-the-Hill and up through
Woldingham to The Ridge, high up on the
North Downs above Oxted.

UMP 227 went on the Historic Commercial
Vehicle Society's annual London to Brighton
run in May 2014. In the picture above, in its
gleaming preserved state, UMP 227 was parked
up on Madeira Drive on Brighton's seafront.

RTW 467

The first of London Transport's 500-strong RTW-class buses, the capital's first 8ft wide double-deck buses, was delivered in 1949 and the last in 1951. The Metropolitan Police were concerned about wider buses being unsuitable for the busy streets of the centre – RTs were 7ft 6in wide – so originally RTWs were not allowed to operate in the central London area, However, following carefully observed trials, that restriction was soon removed.

The RTW chassis, along with the similar 7ft 6in wide RTLs, were built by Leyland and fulfilled London Transport's obligation at the time to source vehicles from manufacturers other than AEC. The chassis was similar to the RTL class but the bodies were all built by Leyland itself, because the cost of changing the jigs set up by the mainstream bodybuilders would have been prohibitive.

In fact, apart from the width, they are a faithful reproduction of the standard RT body, but with just detail differences, including the between-decks band, which is noticeably shallower. The extra six inches' width was taken up by a one-inch wall spacer by each pair of seats and four extra inches for the gangways.

RTWs were allocated initially to Central London routes 6, 6A, 8, 8A, 11, 15, 22, 34B, 46 and 76. Although withdrawn from passenger service between 1964 and 1966, some were kept on as driver-trainers and the final one, RTW185, was sold in 1971.

Route 95 (Cannon Street – Tooting) was the last route operating RTWs and RTW467 ran the final journey on 14 May 1966, thereby ending its 14½ years of LT service. It was bought by a group of well-known London bus enthusiasts and is now owned jointly by Peter, Lord Hendy of Richmond Hill, and Leon Daniels OBE. The bus is still licensed as a Class 6 bus – that is, it is able to carry fare-paying passengers.

On the right, RTW467 was at Tooting on 27 November 1965.

In preservation, the same bus was at Holborn Viaduct at the junction with Newgate Street in April 2014 in the main picture on the opposite page.

Its BESI holders can be seen on the side of the bus, but here without any plates.

The inset detail picture shows RTW467's holders now with the plates inserted, and on the far right is a photograph of one of the roadside scanners.

The small holders on the side of the bus above the canopy were part of the BESI (Bus Electronic Scanning Indicator) system of route regulation and would have had plates inserted.

This system was installed first on route 74 (Camden Town to Putney Heath) in 1958, and later extended to other Central London routes, including 6, 13, 28, 30 and 31. Scanners were located along the route and each bus carried reflective plates with the unique running number in binary code.

The scanner emitted a beam of light which read the plate and the reflection was returned to photo-electric equipment in the scanning head. The position of the bus was transmitted to the central route controllers at the Mansion House Central Division office and displayed there on a screen.

The object of this system was to centralise control and reduce the number of roadside inspectors required.

RF 19

Following the successful trial of prototype AEC Regal IV, UMP 227, London Transport's production run of Regals – the RF class – began delivery in 1951. That was the year of the Festival of Britain and, due to a large influx of visitors to London, there was an urgent need for vehicles better suited to sightseeing and private hire.

This led to the first 25 RF coaches being built specifically for that purpose, with curved windows reaching from the cantrail into the roof. They were also built to the then legal maximum length of 27ft 6in, restricting seating capacity to 35. All RFs that followed were 30ft long, as the legislation had changed.

London Transport marketed an extensive series of sightseeing tours which took the 25 RF coaches, and their fellows in the RFW class, on excursions to such popular venues as Windsor and St Albans, as well as a River Tour which involved taking the coaches across the Thames on the Woolwich Ferry,

10 of these private hire RFs, including RF19, were converted for Green Line use in the mid-1950s. Demand for private hire, and the difficulties London Transport was facing in recruiting driving staff, led to the abandonment of such work and all of the short RFs had been sold by 1963.

RF19 was withdrawn in June 1962 and passed through a number of operators before being bought for preservation by the late Colin Curtis OBE (a former President of the London Bus Museum), who had been heavily involved with the Routemaster development projects and with London Transport as Vehicle Engineering Manager.

It passed through two other preservationists until being acquired by the London Bus Museum in 2012. It went through an extensive restoration process and was relaunched by the Museum in 2019.

The photograph above, taken at a London Bus Museum Spring Gathering, shows the glass roof panels that made these coaches ideal for sightseeing duties.

On the right, RF19 was parked at Stoke Poges to the north of Slough on 2 September 1951 when quite new. The well-known English poem, *Elegy Written in a Country Churchyard*, was penned here by Thomas Gray in 1750.

RFWs

As already mentioned, London Transport needed to renew its private hire fleet in time for the 1951 Festival of Britain. In addition to the first 25 of the new RF class to be used for this purpose, a further 15 coaches on the RF chassis, but with an unusual, straight-lined style of body built by Eastern Coach Works at Lowestoft, were ordered and became the RFW class. These coaches were used for private hire and on advertised excursions. They were only licensed for the tourist season, being stored during the winter.

RFW 14 was sold out of service by London Transport in 1964, and later acquired by noted bus enthusiast, John Marshall. The bus, in good condition both mechanically and internally, has been on loan to the London Bus Museum from his estate. The Museum also has the other survivor from this class, RFW 6, which has been in store awaiting a full restoration, but at the time of writing this has not been a priority.

Above, RFW6 was photographed when new on its way to pick up passengers for a day excursion private hire.

On the right, preserved RFW14 was photographed in Stockwell garage, which opened in April 1952. At that time, it had the largest unsupported roof span in Europe. It was Grade II Listed in 1988.

CONDUCTED COACH TOURS BY LONDON TRANSPORT 1969

There were also five identical coaches supplied to Tilling Transport (BTC) Ltd, the London coach operator in the state-owned BTC group.

Above, Tilling LYM 732 was on Madeira Drive on the seafront at Brighton one warm Sunday evening in June 1953.

However, in 1960 all five were rebodied, the new bodies again being by ECW, but to the design it was then building on the Bristol MW chassis.

The 15 RFWs and these five Tilling coaches were the only vehicles to carry this style of body.

RT 3491

The Green Rover ticket advertised on the side of this bus gave a day's unlimited travel on nearly all London Transport Country Area buses. There was also a Red Rover for Central Area buses. Later on, there was also a higher-priced Golden Rover that allowed travel on Country Area buses and Green Line coaches.

There's more about these tickets on pages 132-133.

Arriving in 1952, RT3491 is a later-built example of the standard RT. All is not what it seems, however. The bus with this bonnet number was always operated in Central Area red livery by London Transport and resided principally at Nunhead, Victoria, Twickenham and Holloway garages. It was withdrawn and sold direct into private preservation in 1973.

At that time London Transport would not allow a bus, once sold, to retain its standard red livery, so RT3491 was repainted green to resemble a Country Area vehicle. It received a complete overhaul at London Bus Museum's old premises at Redhill Road in Cobham and had a larger 11.3-litre engine fitted, which has given it what is best described as a lively performance. It has been extensively used on running days and on bus rides at Brooklands.

Once it was pretty commonplace to see many adverts on the sides of buses for alcohol and cigarettes, and RT3491 in the picture above was sporting a side advert for Black & White whisky and ads either side of the front blinds for Courage beers.

James Buchanan formed his whisky company in 1884, and there's a story that he picked a black Scottie dog and a white Westie (West Highland terrier) as brand mascots after visiting a dog show. They were widely used in advertising and much later appeared on the label of the company's best-selling whisky, Black & White.

RLH 48

Despite London Transport's aspirations for a fully standardised fleet, this was not going to be possible, as it had a number of bus routes in both Central and Country Areas that passed under bridges with insufficient clearance for standard height double-deckers. Its stock of lowbridge buses was war-torn and old-fashioned by the late 1940s and in desperate need of replacement.

Rather than adapt the RT body to meet a lower overall height, London Transport took advantage of a batch of 20 Weymann bodied AEC Regent buses intended for Midland General of Mansfield in Nottinghamshire becoming available, delivery taking place in mid-1950. They had pre-selector gearboxes and air brakes so were, mechanically anyway, RTs with lowbridge bodies.

The RLH was some 1ft 2½ins lower than the standard RT. Of course, a major drawback was the sunken gangway on the offside of the upper deck and four seats across instead of two either side of a central gangway. This meant that passengers had to squeeze past others to gain seats on the nearside; also, the low roof restricted the view out of the windows. Lower deck passengers on the offside had to avoid bumping their heads where the sunken gangway reduced headroom. This initial 20 went to the Country Area in green livery but a further batch of 56 included both green and red examples.

By their very nature, the RLH class was always associated with specific routes, which included the 336 (Chesham-Watford) out of Amersham garage, from where RLH48 started its career, the 410 from Reigate to Bromley via Oxted and the 178 (Stratford local).

RLH48 was withdrawn in 1964 and sold to Whippet Coaches of Hilton, then in Huntingdonshire. In 1974 it was acquired by the LBPT and used extensively for commercial promotional work in the UK and Belgium. 10 years later RLH48 was sold to Richard Proctor, who had memories of travelling on the bus from his Amersham schooldays. Richard repainted it in its original green Country Area livery and restored it to a high standard. RLH48 was a regular performer at running days in the old LT Country Area and was always extremely popular with enthusiasts. After owning the bus for over 30 years, Richard sold it to the London Bus Museum in 2015, where it continues to be a popular bus, with frequent appearances at events.

In the view above RLH48 was on the 178 Stratford local route in Hackney. The bus was on loan to Dalston Central Area garage in late 1959 and early 1960, still in green livery.

The awkwardness of the upstairs seating is obvious in this view of the inside. Single skinning of the roof led to condensation on rainy days.

RF395

The pictures on this page show the pleasing lines and proportions of the Metro-Cammell body for the RFs.

A particularly neat piece of design was the asymmetric front window moulding – cream on buses, pale green on the Green Line version – which surrounded the screen on the nearside but extended backwards on the offside to include the driver's signalling window.

The blind on RF395 in the London Bus Museum on the right was set for the 227 route.

This originally ran from Penge through Bromley and Chislehurst to Eltham and then on to Welling. By the early 1950s, when RFs began running on the route, it had been extended to Crystal Palace at the western end, but only ran to Chislehurst at its eastern end.

Red RFs will always be associated in particular with Kingston, which had a number of single-deck routes fanning out from the town. On the left, RF395 was at Belmont in January 1953.

Another strong association for red RFs was route 210 from Finsbury Park to Highgate and across Hampstead Heath to Golders Green. Single-deckers were used because of this awkward spot at The Spaniards Inn on the Heath, although later double-deckers were allowed. The Spaniards Inn is also featured in the description of TD95 on pages 90-91.

RF395 was photographed recreating the route in RF days on 11 September 2012, exactly 60 years after the 210 became the first Central Area route to be operated with RFs.

The entire class of 700 RFs entered service between 1951 and 1953, which enabled virtually all of the pre-war single-deckers to be withdrawn. A change in legislation since the RF order had been placed allowed the maximum length to be extended to 30 feet. It was too late to change the first 25 private hire versions, but the remaining 675 were all built to this increased length. Over their long service life, the RFs proved to be reliable vehicles.

Many RF buses and coaches were sold off to other operators after withdrawal and a considerable number have survived in preservation, underlining the affection in which they are held, and the build quality and reliability for which the type is known.

RF395 is an example of the red Central Area bus, which differed from the green Country Area buses and Green Line coaches by having no door to the passenger entrance. This was a hangover from the Metropolitan Police's and the Traffic Commissioner's reluctance to allow such 'luxuries' in the name of passenger safety. They argued that the driver or conductor could oversee boarding and alighting, so doors weren't necessary. It didn't do much for passenger and crew comfort in winter months, but they were a hardy lot in those days!

RF395 entered service in January 1953 at Norbiton garage near Kingston, an area always associated with red single-deckers, and particularly RFs until the last ran in 1979. RF395 was withdrawn in 1971 and used by three separate non-commercial organisations, including a Scout troop in Kenton. It was bought for preservation in 1980 and acquired by the London Bus Museum in 2008.

One of the intriguing aspects of bus restoration is the discovery of objects long hidden within the bodywork panels. In RF395's case these included pre-decimal bus tickets and a .303 British Army rifle bullet!

MLL 740

In this picture, BEA coach MLL 740 was at London's Heathrow Airport on 17 October 1967 alongside one of the fully coach-seated AEC Reliances which were also operated by London Transport on behalf of the airline.

The Reliances were used for Executive Express duties, providing a link from check-in at the West London Air Terminal right through to airside, allowing direct access from the coach to the aircraft. This meant they had to have exhaust spark arrestors and amber flashing roof beacons. You can see one of these roof beacons in this view.

From the advent of regular commercial aircraft operations in the late 1920s there developed a need to transport passengers from central London to the airports. Initially, this was at Croydon and the airlines themselves provided the connecting transport by bus or coach and large private car. Some of these services were operated by Tilling on contract to the airlines.

The opening of Northolt, and later Heathrow, airports in West London saw rapid increases in passenger flights to destinations across the world. In turn, this meant a more sophisticated service of connecting bus operations. British European Airways and British Overseas Airways Corporation both operated their own passenger fleets for this purpose. BOAC ran wartime-specification Bedford OWB buses from 1946, which were replaced with Commer Commando and then Rolls-Royce engined Commer-Harrington integral coaches, and ultimately Leyland Atlantean double-deckers.

BEA similarly used Commer Commandos acquired from BOAC. However, BEA later decided not to operate coaches itself but contracted the service from central London terminals (Victoria, Kensington and, ultimately, the West London Air Terminal on Cromwell Road) to London Transport.

London Transport then ran 65 distinctive-looking coaches based on the AEC Regal IV chassis as used for the RF class, but with so-called deck-and-a-half bodies. These could carry 37 passengers, some seated in the raised rear portion, below which was a large luggage compartment. They were delivered in two batches, in 1952 and 1953. Initially, each coach departure from London was specific to a particular flight and the coaches were to be seen heading out to Northolt, and later Heathrow, displaying destinations such as Amsterdam, Brussels, Helsinki, Belgrade, Vienna, etc.

The BEA coaches had low-backed bus-style seats but with deep cushions, making them very comfortable.

On the right, MLL 740 was taking part in the Year of the Bus Cavalcade in 2014, here passing along Parliament Street with the tower of St Margaret's church in the background.

These coaches were replaced in 1966 with a fleet of Routemasters specially built with front entrances, powered doors and towing equipment for luggage trailers. The AEC Regal coaches never received LT bonnet numbers, although on paper they had BEA asset numbers, and were always known by their registration numbers. MLL 740 went direct from London Transport/BEA to the London Bus Preservation Trust in June 1973 and then to member Don Allmey. It is now on loan to the London Bus Museum from the Allmey family.

British European Airways was formed as a division of British Overseas Airways Corporation (BOAC) on 1 January 1946, then as a corporation in its own right on 1 August 1946.

It had flights to Europe, North Africa and the Middle East from airports around the United Kingdom, was the largest UK domestic operator, and operated a network of internal German routes between West Berlin and West Germany as part of the Cold War agreements regulating air travel within Germany.

BEA ceased as a separate legal entity on 1 April 1974, when it was merged with BOAC to form British Airways, which was privatised in February 1987.

GS 34

In the early 1950s there was a further requirement for non-standard buses for Country Area routes which did not require high-capacity vehicles; that was when London Transport's fleet of small C-class pre-war one-man operated buses needed replacing.

Legislation allowed buses with up to 20 seats to be operated by the driver alone and the Cubs had met this requirement. With the Cubs becoming life-expired, London Transport sought a replacement and special dispensation for the seat limit to be increased to 26. The Board's engineers looked at a number of options and eventually chose an unlikely solution in the form of a modified truck chassis from Guy Motors of Wolverhampton with a body built by Eastern Coach Works of Lowestoft. The Guy Vixen chassis was given a bonnet and front wings assembly made by Briggs using pressings from a Ford truck range. Unlike all other London buses of the era, these small vehicles had Perkins P6 diesel engines and 'crash' gearboxes.

A total of 84 were delivered but, right from the start, it was obvious that nothing like that number were actually required. This was an era when private car ownership and family TV viewing was beginning to have a drastic effect on the viability of many rural bus routes for which the GS class had been procured.

From 1963 onwards many of the class were disposed of, with a few surviving to be transferred to London Country Bus Services in January 1970. The last in public service ran on route 336A, connecting the exclusive Loudwater Estate with Rickmansworth Station, which was withdrawn after operation on 29 March 1972.

GS34 was sold out of service by London Transport in 1969 and bought for preservation by a private owner in 1976. It passed to the London Bus Preservation Trust in 1999.

In the picture on the opposite page, GS34 was in Hertford Bus Station on 7 November 1964. The 388 route ran from Harlow through Ware and Hertford to Welwyn.

Above, in preservation, GS34 was photographed at Brooklands on a London Bus Museum open day.

The GSs had Guy Motors' famous 'North American Indian' radiator badge with its 'feathers in our cap' slogan, clearly shown in the picture below.

Many GSs have been preserved, it being a much-loved and fondly-remembered vehicle type. These two, GS42 and GS15 were at Brooklands at the Spring Gathering in 2016.

why were some London buses painted green?

London buses are traditionally thought of as red buses, but there are many preserved London buses which are presented in a green livery, and then there was Green Line as well – more about that on pages 126-127.

During the Victorian era horse-bus operators (the largest of these being the London General Omnibus Company, which was identified by the word GENERAL on the sides of its buses) often grouped together to run particular routes, with common fares. These routes were often identified by different colours for each route. These route-sharing schemes continued into the early years of the 20th century and arrival of the first motorbuses.

By then, one of General's principal competitors was the London Motor Omnibus Company, using the fleet name Vanguard, and its buses were predominantly red. The General took over the Vanguard company in 1908 and continued the use of Vanguard's red livery across its fleet. And ever since that time a central London bus has almost always been in a red livery.

London General continued as the capital's dominant bus operator and, with the increasing reliability of motorbuses, started to run over much longer distances on Sundays and public holidays from London to market towns and popular recreational areas. It also began to acquire bus operators in the Home Counties around London.

During the 1920s London General experienced much competition within London from small independent companies, often with only a few vehicles each, who came to be called 'pirates'.

With increasing road congestion and many different route, vehicle and driver licensing requirements by local authorities and the police in and around London, it was thought by the Government that a significant degree of statutory control should be introduced to manage London's passenger transport efficiently. The London Passenger Transport Act of 1933 created a statutory authority, the London Passenger Transport Board, using the fleet name London Transport to provide local bus, tram and trolleybus services, both within London itself and over an area extending about 30 miles around. The LPTB also took over the Underground and Metropolitan railways (but not the main line railway services in London).

London General was by far the largest bus operator taken over and so the new LPTB bus managers (almost all from London General) continued the red livery for London's buses. For bus operations, the Board created a Central Area (broadly the Metropolitan Police district, or today's Greater London Authority area) and a Country Area which was the ring doughnut-shaped area beyond. Country Area buses were painted in a shade of green, and so preserved London buses from the 1930s to the 1980s can be found painted in red or green, depending on the service history of the bus (or sometimes the owner's whim!). The Country Area management included responsibility for Green Line services.

In 1970 the buses and services in the Country Area were transferred to London Country Bus Services Ltd, a new subsidiary of the National Bus Company, which had come into being a year earlier.

The National Bus Company had been set up by the Labour Government to bring together under one organisation the numerous regional non-municipal bus companies that were under state ownership.

When the Country Area was transferred to the National Bus Company as London Country in 1970, the new company inherited many London-type buses and indeed, more were still being delivered.

London Country's fleet of AEC Merlins didn't fare much better than those in Central London and the suburbs (see pages 140-141). In this picture taken in July 1977, London Country MBS420 was by then in full NBC leaf green with white livery on its way to East Grinstead on the 434, which at this time no longer ran beyond East Grinstead through Dormansland to Edenbridge, as it had done when the RF was working its companion 473 route ten years earlier, shown on the previous page.

Turners Hill, where the picture was taken, is high up in the Sussex Weald. This charming location was also the terminus for two 2-hourly Southdown routes up from Haywards Heath. Passengers were informed they could make connections to Crawley here on the 434 and 473. Few passengers ever did, especially in later years.

Note the London Transport compulsory bus stop here; these were on a white background; a red background was a request stop, as on the picture two pages back. Such stop flags lingered on well after London Transport ceased to operate the services, until they were replaced by the 'national' bus stop design.

Very few remained *in situ* over 50 years since the takeover of LT's Country Area by London Country.

There had been proposals to transfer the Country Area in sections to whichever NBC company it was adjacent to, but working conditions, wages and practices were so different, that too many complexities would have arisen.

In 1986 the Government deregulated bus services outside London and, in due course, London Country Bus Services was split up and privatised. Although this resulted in a number of different companies running the bus routes that had once been Country Area bus routes, several initially stuck to green liveries, even if in different hues and schemes.

In the old Central Area, services eventually became, from 2000, the responsibility of Transport for London (TfL) which today contracts with a number of private bus operators to provide the services as determined by TfL. And, in keeping with tradition, TfL require these operators to use red buses, with which London is associated across the world.

BUS STOPS

I n horse-bus days, passengers were picked up and set down at any point along the route. The passenger could indicate which side of the road to be set down on, so a horse-bus might zig-zag across the roadway from side to side during the journey. This traffic hazard was dealt with by the Metropolitan Streets Act of 1867, which now required the horse-bus driver to draw in to the left-hand side of the road only to pick up and set down passengers. Before this, it was usual for the entrance/exit of the bus to be at the back; now the entrance/exit could be on the rear nearside, where it remained for over a hundred years through to the end of Routemaster bus operation.

At important road junctions and stations, passengers would congregate to board or alight at a point on the pavement, as there were no bus stops erected to confirm exactly where to wait. London General sought to introduce fixed stopping places at certain points from 1913, but had very little success. It is recorded that by 1919 there were just 59 bus stops with posts and flags compared to some 19,000 in the Transport for London area in the 21st century. Trams were required by legislation to have fixed stopping places, but not buses. However, in 1920 London General tried again, and a number of fixed stops were erected. It experimented with different types and shapes for the 'flags', and an early popular choice was the style known as 'the tombstone'. An example of one of these is on display in the London Bus Museum.

Fixed stops improved the regulation of bus services, were convenient for passengers and achieved efficiency, so in March 1935, as an experiment, fixed stops were introduced along the roads between Euston and Seven Sisters. This was considered so successful that it was decided to introduce fixed stops throughout the Central (red bus) Area, and in much of the Country (green bus) Area.

The stops were either 'compulsory' or 'voluntary' (later called 'request') stops and so a very considerable number of bus stop flags needed to be designed, constructed and erected in a short time. Hans Schleger was commissioned by Frank Pick of the LPTB in 1935 to design the new flags and he created a design that is simple, clear, elegant, immediately recognisable, adaptable . . . and timeless.

Schleger (1898–1976) was born in Germany and he and his wife chose to move to London in 1932, where he worked as a graphic designer. His classic London bus stop design was the famous roundel on a background that was white, red or green (for compulsory, request and Green Line stops) with the words Bus Stop or Coach Stop in black Johnston typeface across the bar of the roundel. The design was a classic, and as developed and adapted, is still in use today. Some examples are shown here and are part of a large collection on display at the London Bus Museum.

The small plates listing routes at any particular bus stop are known as E plates. Once enamel, these are now adhesive vinyl. The enamel plates have become very collectable, some commanding high prices.

The selection below includes an ordinary bus route plate indicating a fare stage (where incremental fares along the route would increase), a Green Line plate with destinations and an express route plate.

Illustrated top right are the main designs of bus stop flags in the days of London Transport with, at the bottom, a more recent Transport for London incarnation.

On the right is a London General 'tombstone' and a much more recent London bus stop. In busy locations today not all buses at the same location can use the same stop, so there'll be several, each lettered, and a plan to show which route stops at each stop.

There is now no real distinction in London between Compulsory and Request stops – all stops on the line of route are now treated as compulsory inasmuch as the bus must stop if a passenger appears to be waiting or if the bell has been rung, but if neither condition applies then the driver may continue past the stop. Previously, compulsory stops required the driver to stop regardless.

RT4825

Numerically the last of the RT family, RT4825 was delivered new to London Transport in March 1954 and entered service at Cricklewood garage. Like all RTs it went through chassis and body changes at overhaul, ending up being used as a driver training bus between 1971 and 1976.

The significance of the bonnet number was recognised when the bus was withdrawn and it went through a final overhaul at Aldenham before being transferred to London Transport's historic vehicle collection. It has spent several years on public display at the London Transport Museum at Covent Garden.

In the picture above, the highest numbered RT was posed alongside the lowest numbered RT on Wisley Airfield at a London Bus Museum gathering.

On the left, on 10 October 1965 during its years in revenue-earning service, RT4825 was inside Shepherd's Bush garage.

The name of Prince Marshall features in the history of a number of the buses in this book. In particular, he had much involvement in the acquisition and initial restorations of the 1925 Dennis open-top double-decker D142, the 1929 AEC single-decker T31, the 1930 AEC 'Thomas Tilling' double-decker ST922, and the RT prototype, the 1939 RT1.

Prince Marshall (Prince was his given name) died in November 1981 at the early age of 44, following a long period of treatment for sickle-cell anaemia and an unsuccessful kidney transplant.

When not yet 20, he was one of the small group who purchased T31 from London Transport in 1956. Another of that small group was Michael Dryhurst, who, under the imprint Dryhurst Publications, published books, the first of which was *The London Bus 1933-1957*, co-authored by Prince and published in 1957. In 1962 Prince began publication of *Vintage Commercial* magazine and, shortly after, at the beginning of 1963, he first published *Old Motor* magazine.

They were published under the imprint of North London Artists, but it proved a little too ambitious to publish two separate magazines and within a few months they had been combined as *Old Motor and Vintage Commercial*. Prince was also an early Chairman of the London Bus Preservation Group, later the London Bus Preservation Trust.

Starting in the summer months of 1972, and continuing in the summers of 1973, 1977 and 1978, Prince worked ST922 on a West End route numbered 100 (the exact route taken varied each year); then in 1980, when the London Transport Museum opened in Covent Garden, route 100 was reinstated, running from Covent Garden to Oxford Circus, and the buses used included D142, ST922 and RT1. Obsolete Fleet was the name given by Prince to this business, which also included Round London sightseeing tours using Daimler Fleetlines which were ex-London Transport, and D9 double-deckers which had originated with Midland Red. Sadly, the Obsolete Fleet business did not long survive after Prince's death, and was wound up in 1983.

Prince Marshall

Taken at Barking garage on 7 April 1979, this picture shows Prince Marshall with RT1 at the celebration for the last day of operation of RT buses in London service.

London bus driver

landmarks 1

Joe Clough

Joseph (Joe) Clough is remembered for being London's first black bus driver. He was born in Kingston in Jamaica in 1885, and worked as a stable hand for a Scottish doctor on the island. Joe's employer moved to England in 1906 and Joe agreed to go with him and work for him in London. The doctor acquired an early motor-car, which Joe learned to drive, and he became the doctor's chauffeur.

Joe Clough joined the London General Omnibus Company in 1910, training as a driver at Shepherd's Bush garage on one of the early motorbuses. He became a regular driver on route 11. He married Millicent in 1911 and shortly before the outbreak of the First World War left London General and moved to Bedfordshire.

He volunteered as an ambulance driver on the Western Front between 1915 and 1919 and later drove for a Bedford bus company, retiring from bus driving in 1947 and later becoming a taxi driver. He died in 1976.

In 1956 London Transport was invited to Barbados to recruit bus conductors. Successful candidates received interest-free loans to travel to the UK. Upon arrival in the UK they received two weeks' training before starting work. Many were upset by the colder climate and experienced racism but joining local churches and the LT Sports and Social Club helped them settle into life in the UK.

Many subsequently qualified as drivers and the picture on the far right shows Earl Gibson, from Barbados, in a photograph he had taken after passing out as a driver in 1962. Earl (left), accompanied by Sophia Gibson, his daughter, and another driver, Ruel Mosely (centre), are in this colour picture to the right on a visit to the London Bus Museum in 2022.

London Transport recruited just under 4,000 employees for bus and Underground services from Barbados, and later from Jamaica and Trinidad, until recruiting from the West Indies ceased in 1970.

Jill Viner

London bus driver
landmarks 2

Jill Viner (1952-1996) is remembered as London's first woman bus driver. She obtained her bus driving licence in June 1974, the year in which the law changed and women were permitted to drive buses in service carrying passengers. She worked on routes from Norbiton bus garage. Jill had wanted to be a bus driver from an early age and at the time said, *"I've always been interested in buses – don't ask me why. I was about 8 years old when I made up my mind to be a bus driver."* The first woman commercial jet pilot in the UK had qualified two years earlier, in 1972.

In the years before the First World War there were very few women employed by London's bus operators – and they were employed in clerical and cleaning jobs. With so many men leaving for war service, for the first time women began to be recruited as conductors and a Mrs G Duncan is reported to have started work as the first London bus 'conductress' in 1915. But after the end of the war, as men were de-mobilised and returned to their previous employment, all the conductresses, by then nicknamed clippies, had been dismissed and replaced by men by the early 1920s.

The news stories in 1974 of Jill's successful employment as a London bus driver encouraged a few other women to apply for a bus driver licence, and in 1980 London Transport began to actively seek to recruit women drivers. In March 2014, the London Mayor's office reported that of London's then 24,500 bus drivers about 7% were women.

Routemaster
a London icon

how the Routemaster
came about and why it is such
a much-loved legend

To the public at large, any red double-deck bus with engine at the front, separate driver's cab and rear entrance (usually without doors) manufactured within the past 75 years is a Routemaster. Many will not be Routemasters and this book shows some surviving examples of the RT class of London buses, manufactured between 1939 and 1954 in greater numbers than the Routemaster.

The Routemaster itself was the last traditional London double-deck bus, and was a continuum of a style of motor bus first developed at the beginning of the 20th century. The mechanical sub-frame assemblies were made by AEC in Southall, Middlesex, and then sent to Park Royal Vehicles in North West London for the body to be built and sub-frames attached. There was a great deal of engineering and styling input from London Transport's own engineers. Engines were supplied mostly by AEC (although Leyland supplied several hundred as original equipment, too) and almost all of them that survive have been re-engined more than once with more modern units. (Peter, Lord Hendy of Richmond Hill owns a Routemaster now fitted with the latest Euro-6 engine which meets London's current Ultra-Low Emission Zone standards.)

London's bus types had traditionally been referred to by a letter code, the first of which was the X-type in 1909. How some of these letters were derived was never clear, and what the letters stood for has never been officially stated, but until the Routemaster they never had official names. The Routemaster (coded RM) was therefore unusual in being given a name by which the general public would refer to the bus. Whether it would have achieved iconic status otherwise is open to doubt. The name came shortly before the prototype bus was first shown to the public in 1954, and appears to have originated with one or more of the senior executives in London Transport. But whoever came up with the name, it was an inspired choice.

The Routemaster later became available on the open market. Northern General in Gateshead bought 50, although in due course second-hand examples came to be operated all over the country (and in some instances, abroad as well). One reason for its failure to attract other customers when new was that it was relatively expensive to buy.

The first Routemaster bus entered service in 1956, and the last was delivered in 1968. A total of 2,876 were manufactured (including FRM1), most in red livery for London Transport's Central Area, initially to replace trolleybuses, although there were 100 green long Routemasters for the Country Area and 111 Green Line coach versions in both standard and extended lengths. British European Airways also took 65 Routemasters, painted in its livery but operated on behalf of BEA by London Transport. These carried passengers and their luggage (transported in a trailer behind the bus) between the West London Air Terminal in Kensington and Heathrow Airport. The Northern General and BEA buses had a forward entrance with doors, instead of the open rear platform, as did one prototype (RMF1254) constructed for experimental use and later sold to Northern General.

It could be argued that the Routemaster design was already obsolete when the first one appeared. Manufacturers were already beginning to experiment with moving the engine to the rear, and the first British commercially successful bus of that type was the Leyland Atlantean, which first went into service in Glasgow, Wallasey and South Wales at the end of 1958.

London Transport at this time was of the view that the traditional double-decker with a driver and conductor and incorporating the latest technical improvements would continue to be the most suitable bus for London. Only in 1965 did it buy its first Leyland Atlantean and Daimler Fleetline equivalents and at the end of 1966 London Transport put into service a rear-engined, front-entrance Routemaster prototype, FRM 1, constructed mostly from standard Routemaster parts, but this bus remained a one-off.

London Transport's reasons for preferring the Routemaster at this time included:

- an open rear platform for speedier boarding and alighting in London's busy urban environment
- aluminium construction that made it relatively light for improved fuel consumption
- being suited to its established, efficient production line overhaul system at Aldenham

At Aldenham each bus body was separated from the chassis, and both then moved through the works separately. Necessary parts were refurbished or replaced until a body and chassis were reunited, but not usually in the same combination as when they entered the works. The Routemaster was designed with this overhaul system in mind. The Routemaster did not have a chassis as such: there was an A frame at the front carrying the engine, steering column, front suspension, pedal gear and front axle, and a B frame at the rear carrying the rear axle and suspension.

Continuing labour shortages were becoming a problem for London Transport as the 1960s progressed, and the move to one-person operation took place where possible, with the driver taking fares and issuing tickets. The Transport Act of 1968 at last permitted the operation of double-deck buses by the driver alone, and also introduced bus grants offering a 25% subsidy (later increased to 50%) to bus operators buying standard buses suitable for one-person operation. Therefore, the Routemaster was becoming increasingly anachronistic.

The Routemaster easily exceeded its original design life and the first significant withdrawals of these buses in London took place in the 1980s. Notwithstanding the need for a two-person crew, there were many bus operators in the UK who were happy to acquire these now iconic, well-maintained buses. However, many of the buses bought to replace the Routemaster, such as the DMS-class Daimler Fleetlines, were considered unsuitable for London and its traffic conditions and were withdrawn, leaving the surviving Routemasters to be refurbished and continue in service. Some were converted to open top and put on London Transport's own Round London Sightseeing Tours.

Ken Livingstone became Mayor of London in 2000 and was very much in favour of continuing Routemaster operation, which led to some 50 Routemasters, which had previously been sold out of London service, being re-purchased for use in London after refurbishment. But from 2003, Transport for London (TfL) recommended its plans to end the use of conductors in London, and so sales of Routemasters took place once more. As well as saving costs by having one-person operation, it was important to move toward an all low-floor bus fleet, the Routemaster never being accessible by wheelchair users. On 9 December 2005 the last Routemasters in regular London service came off the road, although a few continued to operate in London service on heritage/tourist routes on behalf of TfL until September 2019.

But if the Routemaster no longer operates regular bus services in London, an astonishing number have survived and can be seen not only in London, but around the UK, and indeed the world. Over 1,200 of the 2,876 constructed exist in one form or another today. Some may be static, without engines, as glamping buses or B&Bs and some may be in need of restoration, but a very large number are operational. Privately-owned and museum Routemasters may be seen, and ridden on, at heritage bus running days and bus museum event days throughout the UK, including the annual bus service on a Saturday in August across Salisbury Plain to the abandoned village of Imber on roads closed to the public for military training purposes for most of the year.

Other Routemasters are available for private hire for weddings and other party events, and they can be found as playbuses, showrooms, bars, food courts, sightseeing buses, grandstands at the Derby, and are used for tea-time tours and ghost tours. And, of course, as film and TV production extras – nothing sets a scene in London like a red Routemaster bus (even if not correct for the period being portrayed!).

None of this could possibly have been foreseen when the prototype first appeared before the public in 1954. The Routemaster's longevity has been, and continues to be, a remarkable story.

Below is RML2344 in the lonely wilds of Salisbury Plain on the annual Imberbus run, where hordes of Routemasters, and a few other preserved buses, convey hundreds of people across roads that normally only see rabbits and tanks. This day out raises money for charity and is enormous fun.

Opposite at the bottom you can see the contrast in bonnet styling between the prototype RM2, which was delivered in green Country Area livery and production RML883. These were at the Routemaster 60 celebrations in Finsbury Park in 2014.

RM1

In its original form, RM1's radiator was under the floor behind the driver to keep the overall length to the then permitted 27 feet.

In this form on its first trials in service on route 2, RM1 was turning into Victoria from the top of Vauxhall Bridge Road on 9 February 1956 in this picture.

Without doubt, the Routemaster epitomises the London bus beloved of traditionalists and tourists alike. It worked the streets of London from 1956 until 2005 and may still be seen across the world as tourist buses, bars, mobile offices and in many other varied uses. Many have been preserved and are kept by museums, private individuals and commercial operators, all bringing recognition and enjoyment.

Development of the bus which became known as the Routemaster started even before the last RT types were being delivered. The design brief was for a bus which would provide private car-style comfort for passengers, improved working environments for the crew and ease of maintenance and overhaul for the engineers.

RM1 was launched in 1954 and spent two years on trial before entering public service. Together with the other three prototypes it was modified later to replicate the frontal design which had been agreed for the production vehicles. Ironically, it is the only one not to have been returned to original condition by preservationist owners. It was strange that, for such a significant bus, it was sold in 1973 to Lockheed for braking trials. It was bought back by London Transport in 1981 and placed in the London Transport Museum collection. It has since been used regularly for passenger carrying duties, having been fully certified for such use.

The maximum length of 2-axle double-deckers had been increased to 27ft 6ins during the development of RM1, and since RM1 had been prone to overheating, the opportunity was taken to move the radiator to the front to solve this problem. On the left you can see the changed lower frontal appearance of RM1. RM2 was near identical to this.

RM1 later still was modified to match the production versions and remained like this into preservation. Above it was in Golders Green on the route 2 commemorative run on 7 February 2016, with the famous Hippodrome theatre behind it.

The Golders Green Hippodrome was built in 1913 as a 3,000-seat music hall but was taken over by the BBC in the 1960s as a television studio, and later became used as an evangelical church.

RML 3

The third Routemaster prototype carried Leyland running units in a body built by Weymann at Addlestone in Surrey. It was taken into stock in July 1957, but didn't actually enter passenger revenue earning service until 1959, and then only briefly, to be relegated to driver training duties until it was sold in 1974.

The London Bus Preservation Trust acquired the bus direct from London Transport and it became the first Routemaster to be preserved. Museum volunteers rebuilt the front end to its original design in time for the RM50 event at Finsbury Park in 2004.

During its brief life in service on the capital's streets, RML3 was photographed heading west along Oxford Street by Oxford Circus Station in the picture at the foot of the opposite page.

The rest are views of it in preservation. In the night shot above, RML3 was by Whitehall Court in Horse Guards Avenue in September 2019.

On the left RML3 was the third one in at the RM50 event in Finsbury Park. The buses were skilfully lined up starting with the lowest numbered (RM1), here with its bonnet open.

Between RM1 and RML3 is RM2 on its first public outing since its restoration from red back to its original Country Area green livery, which it wore for only three months following introduction into service in 1957.

The interior shot at the top of the opposite page was taken on the route 93 running day in 2021.

The fourth Routemaster prototype was designed as a coach which could upgrade certain Green Line routes to enhance capacity, while providing closer to car-style comfort to entice car travellers onto Green Line for trips into the centre of London or, conversely, out into London's countryside. This Routemaster was given the number CRL4.

London Transport, and even London General in the earliest days of Green Line, had considered specially-designed double-deck coaches for Green Line. For example, in 1931 a 6-wheel LT-class AEC Renown double-decker, LT1137, was built but wasn't successful in service. Then in 1937, a side-engined AEC Q double-decker, Q188, appeared as a prototype for a fleet of similar coaches, but this was not to be and the vehicle was relegated to Country Area local bus services. During and immediately after the Second World War, standard double-decker buses in Green Line colours had worked on the more heavily-used services, but had no special features, nor offered any greater comfort than normal buses.

After the war, London Transport converted one of the first RTs, RT97, into a rather stylish, quite rakish, Green Line coach with more luxurious trim, becoming RTC1. The coach was mechanically unreliable but some of its features formed part of the development work for this coach Routemaster. RTC1 only worked on Green Line services for nine months, being then demoted to bus work. Thus it was in Epsom on 7 August 1950 in the picture at the top of the next page, on its way to Chessington Zoo. Meantime, standard RT-type buses in Green Line colours regularly worked Green Line routes in East London from Aldgate into Essex in the 1950s and early 1960s.

CRL4 entered service in 1957 and, unlike the other three Routemaster prototypes, had a reasonably full service life as a coach, and later as a bus with London Country, principally from Hatfield garage. Its earlier bonnet assembly and grille had been exchanged for the standard later RMC style with twin headlights and it was renumbered RMC4, too. Latterly, it was used frequently for 'last rites' duties on abandoned Green Line routes, for staff on retirement day, and for attendance at bus rallies.

CRL4 was bought by Roger Wright (owner of the London Bus Company and the Epping Ongar Railway) and eventually it emerged from store with its radiator grille area restored to the original appearance.

In its early days, CRL4 spent six months working the 711 route between High Wycombe and Reigate. It was pulling away from the forecourt of Uxbridge Station in the picture below passing an Austin A40 Somerset with an early Standard Vanguard Estate Car outside Mac Fisheries.

Mac Fisheries used to be in just about every town in the late 1950s. But as frozen fish products were introduced to consumers, sales of wet fish began to decline, and the last Mac Fisheries shops closed in 1979.

GREEN LINE
LONDON TRANSPORT

S ome of the vehicles featured in this book are in the green livery of Green Line coaches, a brand which has changed and evolved over the years.

With the increasing mechanical reliability of motor coaches in the 1920s, many regular timetabled coach services were introduced throughout the country by both large and small companies. They were run as express routes with limited stops. Also, there were no local fares, so short-distance passengers were not catered for.

Some required pre-booking, while on others tickets could be bought on board. London was of course the destination of many of these services, and London's principal bus operator at the time, the London General Omnibus Company, began running express coach services in the late 1920s between Central London and a number of important towns up to about 30 miles from London.

During the 1950s and 1960s, three Green Line routes ran north from Dorking, all operated with the ubiquitous RF single-deckers, as were most Green Line routes then.

The 712 and 713 went to Dunstable and the 714 to Luton. In this picture on the right from the mid-1960s, RF228 was preparing to leave the bus station on the forecourt of Dorking garage, where this RF was based. Conductors were still employed on Green Line services then.

In July 1930 London General formed a new company, Green Line Coaches Limited, to operate these services, which then had eight routes and some 60 vehicles, all under the name Green Line and in a green livery. The vehicles were generally standard single-deck buses but with more luxurious seating, better interior trim and luggage racks.

Introducing new routes and acquiring the services of competitors enabled the Green Line network to grow rapidly, and many routes were linked together through Central London, so that by the mid-1930s most Green Line services ran from a town at the extremity of London Transport's operating area on one side of London through to another on the opposite side.

With the formation of the London Transport Passenger Board in 1933, Green Line was managed by London Transport's Country Area division and new vehicles were introduced over the next few years. Green Line services were suspended during World War II, but reinstated from 1946, with routes reorganised and now numbered in a series starting from 701. Most routes still ran across Central London, and were operated by single-deck vehicles.

The first Green Line route which did not pass through central London at all was the 725, introduced in 1953 between Windsor and Gravesend via Kingston and Croydon. In the first half of the 1960s, double-deck Routemaster coaches were built for use on some Green Line routes; then in 1970, with the formation of the Greater London Council and it taking control of London's bus and tube services, the Country Area was passed to the National Bus Company, itself only formed the year before. London Country was the company now responsible for Green Line.

The Green Line network was struggling by then and throughout the 1970s patronage continued to decline. Increasing car use, improved and electrified rail services, traffic congestion and changing social habits all contributed to this, and the last cross-London routes soon ended. With reduced frequencies and a number of routes withdrawn, it looked as though it might be the end for this once proud name.

But following deregulation of coach services in 1980, a new policy was implemented and the Green Line network expanded outside its traditional area, reaching Brighton, Cambridge, Northampton and Oxford, and services to London's airports (Heathrow, Gatwick, Stansted and Luton) became an increasing focus of operations.

With modern true coaches too, as opposed to enhanced buses, Green Line seemed to be entering a new phase, but gradually the market evaporated again and, following the break-up of London Country and subsequent sale of its component parts to the private sector, ownership of the Green Line name became fragmented.

By 2022 the only routes marketed as Green Line were those operated by Reading Buses, predominantly between London, Slough, Windsor and Legoland, and by Arriva between Heathrow and Harlow via St Albans, and from Luton Airport into London.

In the picture above, although superficially looking like a genuine pre-war scene of a 10T10-type Green Line coach lit up inside at twilight, this scene was an Ensignbus running day and the coach Ensign's beautifully preserved T499.

The roof route boards were a distinguishing feature of Green Line coaches from the earliest days right up until the late 1960s.

Top right is Arriva the Shires 4049 in one of the later incarnations of the Green Line livery.

Reading Buses painted some of its double-deck buses used on the London to Windsor and Legoland service into this dramatic livery in the picture immediately above. It was another Best Impressions Green Line creation.

The map on the right shows the Green Line network as it was in 1965. Although the south orbital 725 was in operation then, the north orbital 724 was yet to be introduced.

RM140

A standard production model, RM140 entered service from Walthamstow garage in February 1960 on routes 58, 256 and 257. The very earliest Routemasters could be recognised by virtue of their non-opening front upper deck windows. It was planned that opening windows would not be needed at the front because the advanced heating and ventilation system would cope with air circulation and prevent them from steaming up.

Unfortunately, this did not prove to be the case in practice and very soon all deliveries came with quarter-drop openers. As bodies became swapped around during the overhaul process, the early bodies were to be found on later numbered buses and vice versa. RM140 had body number B1572 in 1968, which had opening windows. A further body swap in 1980 gave RM140 another earlier body, which it kept.

Many of the early Routemasters had issues with their unique hydraulic braking systems and were taken off the road for rectification. This could have been rather embarrassing for London Transport, given the extensive publicity around the advent of the Routemaster.

RM140 was withdrawn in 1984 and, like many other Routemasters, found its way into preservation. Having passed through the hands of several private owners, it was acquired by the London Bus Preservation Trust in 2012. It is in original condition, having been retrofitted with the early style of radiator grille, tungsten interior lighting, brake cooling vents and a maroon interior.

With the distinctive nose of the supersonic aircraft Concorde, one of the many displays at Brooklands, in the background, preserved RM140 was at a London Bus Museum event in the picture on the opposite page.

Above, RM140 was in Lewisham Bus Station on 14 August 1982 working the 94 route southwards to Bromley and Orpington. This route number was later used for the western section of the 88 when that route was split in Central London.

The bus on the far right was a Scania Metropolitan, built jointly by MCW and Scania between 1973 and 1978 and based on Scania's BR111DH chassis.

London Transport had the largest number of Metropolitans, with 164 being delivered between 1975 and 1977, but by 1983 all had been withdrawn. The Metropolitan was replaced by the Metrobus, of which London Transport ordered 1,440 of the first version – see pages 144-145.

RMCs

The trials of prototype Green Line Routemaster CRL4 (later redesignated RMC4) were successful, so 68 coach versions of the production Routemaster were ordered. These were delivered in 1962 and put into service on a number of Green Line routes with high loadings. On some routes, like the 715 between Guildford and Hertford, London Transport justified a not very customer-friendly reduction in frequency by claiming the service still offered at least the same number of seats per hour.

The coaches were fitted out to a high standard with the idea that passengers might be coaxed out of their cars or from the parallel railway services which, in those days, were perceived as slow and unreliable.

On the left is RMC1461 in the Beckton Express red and gold livery.

The main picture on the left shows RMC1461 in London Country days in the 1970s, demoted to bus work and wearing National Bus Company leaf green livery.

On the right, RMC1469 was also photogrphed in London Country days still in original London Transport Lincoln green but with a yellow band and the London Country name in yellow capitals.

Below, back in Green Line colours, it was at Stonecot Hill in Sutton on 10 August 2008 while in the ownership of vintage bus operators Greene Lane.

They had air suspension at the rear, 57 seats with deeper cushions, luggage racks, platform doors, fluorescent lighting and twin headlamps. As such, they were very comfortable vehicles to ride in. A nice touch was a raised metal Green Line roundel on the upper sides.

The Routemaster coaches passed to London Country when the Country Area (which operated Green Line services) was transferred to the National Bus Company in 1970. In the mid-1970s they were downgraded to buses and in many cases replaced by less comfortable, one-person operated Leyland National single-deckers.

The London Bus Museum has two examples of the RMC – RMC1461 and RMC1469. Both of these had been sold off by London Country. RMC 1461 was bought back by London Transport in 1979, and in 1989 was refurbished and painted in red with gold lining for an express service from London's redeveloping Docklands to Aldwych via the City. The route was given the number X15 and was known as the Beckton Express. This route was taken off in 1995; the bus had meanwhile been repainted into Green Line livery and used in normal service and for private hire by Stagecoach. It was withdrawn from service in 2003 and kindly donated to the London Bus Museum, and has since been repainted into the red Beckton Express livery, as in the upper picture on the opposite page.

RMC 1469 had been used in 1964 as a trial for some bodywork changes that London Transport wanted to introduce on the longer RCL class of Routemaster Green Line coaches – in particular, a wider front number and via point screen and a revised front grille. London Transport repurchased the bus, along with others, in 1980 and, having painted it into red livery, used it as a driver recruitment and training bus. In 1999 the bus was acquired for preservation and re-painted into Green Line livery.

Kept in very good condition, the bus was acquired by the London Bus Museum in 2021 from the Estate of Bill Ackroyd, a long-time member of the London Bus Museum and former Chairman of the Isle of Wight Bus Museum.

red & green rovers

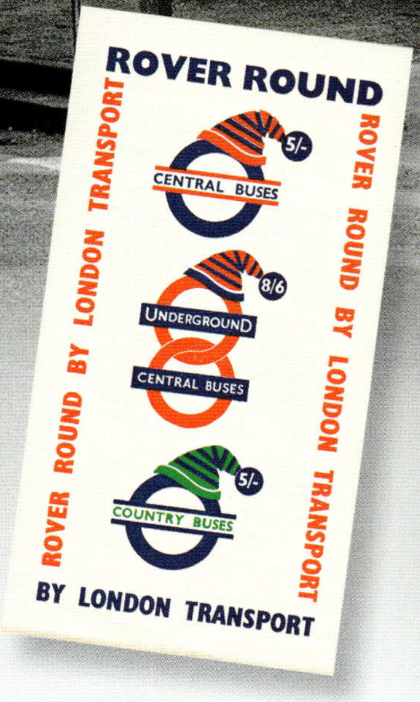

With a Green Rover, if planned well, you could get to the extremities of the Country Area, such as East Grinstead in the picture above.

This shot was taken in late 1965, just after the eight experimental XF-class Park Royal bodied Daimler Fleetlines had entered the fleet and been put to work, initially on the 424 route between East Grinstead and Reigate via Horley.

On the far right, a green RF was heading through wooded Kentish hills on its way to Westerham near Hosey Hill, not far from Chartwell, in the mid-1960s.

Well remembered by bus enthusiasts of a certain age, Red Rovers and Green Rovers were tickets allowing unlimited travel for a day on, respectively, Central Area red bus services and Country Area green bus services. Many a young enthusiast discovered the geography of inner London, the outer suburbs and much of the Home Counties with these tickets. Until they were introduced, exploring far by bicycle might be too difficult or tiring in a day, and purchase of individual tickets for each journey would exhaust the change in your pocket.

With today's London bus passes and tickets available for purchase instantly on your phone, or by using a credit or debit card, it is perhaps difficult now to remember the novelty of the unlimited opportunity opened up by these tickets to roam far and wide by London Transport buses. And the young enthusiasts of the 1950s and 1960s have now reached the age at which they can continue to explore with their 'Older Person's Bus Pass' or their Freedom Pass – unimagined all those years ago.

The expert on London's bus tickets over the years is Laurie Akehurst, who has kindly verified information in this chapter. The Red Rover ticket was introduced from Saturday 12 October 1957 at a cost of 5/- for adults, and 2/6 (half-a-crown) for children. They were available on a Saturday or a Sunday only, and could be bought from most Underground stations, from the offices of agents of Victoria Coach Station and from certain London Transport Enquiry Offices. For the day chosen, from midnight to midnight you had unlimited travel on Central Area bus and trolleybus routes. The tickets could be bought on the day, or in advance from the previous Monday. During the month of August 1961 the tickets, rebranded as Bus-About, were also available to be used on any day between Monday and Friday after 9.30am.

From March 1962 the cost of the tickets increased to 6/- and 3/-, and could now also be bought at Central Area bus garages. For 1962, and from 1964 onwards, the tickets also became available for use on Mondays to Fridays before 9.30am during July, August and September (for 1963 this was restricted to August only). The price increased again from June 1968, to 7/- and 3/6. It would seem that from September 1969 the Red Rover ticket was available on any day (but still only after 9.30am on Mondays to Fridays), and the price continued to increase.

From the beginning of 1970 the tickets were again re-branded, this time to Red Bus Rover, and by the beginning of 1972 (and after decimalisation of the currency) the prices were 50 pence and 25 pence. The design of the tickets changed over the years, and eventually, with the introduction of zoned fare systems and a variety of passes and travelcards, the Red Rover became unnecessary; they were discontinued from 21 January 1986, by which time the prices were £2 for adults and 60p for children.

The Green Rover ticket was introduced a little before the Red Rover. They could be bought in the Country Area South from Sunday 20 May 1956, and in the Country Area North from 1 July 1956, and were available on all London Transport's Country Area (green) bus routes, but not Green Line services. There were a few exceptions where they could not be used, such as hospital services, buses of other operators running joint services with London Transport, buses which operated under running powers running beyond the original LPTB Area (such as between Tring and Aylesbury) and – until April 1960 – in the Grays area. The price on introduction of the ticket was 5/- for adults and 2/6 for children, increasing in March 1962 (in line with Red Rover tickets) to 6/- and 3/-.

When originally introduced they were referred to as Rover Tickets. It was not until the Red Rover had been introduced that they were designated Green Rovers – the earliest item of publicity calling them Green Rovers was printed in June 1958. They could only be bought from the conductor (or driver on one-person operated buses) and not at garages or London Transport Enquiry Offices. They were available seven days a week, but were only valid after 9.30am on Mondays to Saturdays, although the Saturday restriction was removed from July 1961, as fewer people now worked a half-day on Saturdays.

The Green Rover price continued to increase in line with Red Rovers until 1968, but from January 1970, after the Country Bus Area became separated from London Transport, the Green Rover ticket price, set now by London Country Bus Services, increased regularly and by October 1975 was 75p for adults and 38p for children. The Green Rover ticket was finally discontinued from the end of 1976.

Many an enthusiast took full advantage of the Red Rover and Green Rover tickets and, armed with a notebook, pencil, the latest Ian Allan ABC London Transport bus number book, a bus map, maybe a timetable, and a couple of sandwiches and a bottle of Tizer, would have had glorious days travelling on the buses.

With the generally lower frequencies of Country Area routes, you had to make sure that, as the day progressed, you were going to be able to get back to your starting point before your parents would start to get anxious about you. There were no mobile phones in those days.

PRE-DECIMAL CURRENCY		DECIMAL EQUIVALENT
2/6	2 shillings & 6 pence (half a crown)	12½p
3/-	3 shillings	15p
3/6	3 shillings & 6 pence	17½p
5/-	5 shillings	25p
6/-	6 shillings	30p
7/-	7 shillings	35p

FRM 1

London persisted with the traditional crew-operated rear-entrance double-decker when, from the mid-1960s, most provincial bus operators had adopted the front-entrance, rear-engined double-decker as the norm. The longevity of the Routemaster was closely linked to London Transport's overhaul system and the undisputed data on boarding and alighting times at bus stops, for which the open rear platform was best suited.

With such heavy commitment to the traditional Routemaster, London Transport was not over-enthusiastic about converting to rear-engined double-deckers but, eventually, was persuaded to try out such designs in the mid-1960s. It bought 50 Leyland Atlanteans and eight Daimler Fleetlines – all with Park Royal bodywork – which initially were crew-operated. In a vain bid to couple the successful Routemaster style of integral construction with the modern front-entrance, rear-engine concept, London Transport with Park Royal Vehicles built its own rear-engined Routemaster. FRM1, as it was called, used 60% standard Routemaster parts in its construction but suffered technical problems, particularly with the complex heating and ventilation system, which were never fully resolved.

FRM1 remained a one-off, despite parts being produced which would have enabled two further buses to be built. Development costs, and the already relatively high production cost of the standard Routemaster compared with other manufacturers' products, plus a degree of consolidation within the manufacturing industry, finally saw off the project.

Despite all of the above, FRM1 had a reasonably useful service life. It entered traffic on route 76 from Tottenham in June 1967. It was subsequently used on the 233/234 local routes in Croydon. After overhaul it went to Potters Bar for local route 284, and then to Stockwell garage for the Round London Sightseeing Tour.

In 1983 FRM1 was transferred to London Transport Museum stock and sent to Acton Depot. It was used for a commemorative tour of its Croydon area routes for the London Transport Museum Friends in December 2019.

Above, FRM1 was at Roundshaw on 24 January 1970 when working the Croydon local routes 233/234.

The colour pictures show FRM1 in preservation, on 22 June 2014 in Lower Regent Street approaching Piccadilly Circus for the Year of the Bus cavalcade, its distinctive rear profile and the unusual but neat rear downstairs seating arrangement.

RML2760

Routemaster production continued right up to 1968 when the last, and highest numbered bus, RML2760, was delivered and went into service from Upton Park garage on route 15.

The integral construction of the Routemaster, with its separate front and rear mechanical assemblies, enabled the vehicle to be lengthened to 30ft simply by inserting an extra half-bay into the bodywork and using a longer propshaft, thus increasing seating capacity from 64 to 72. A trial batch of extended buses went into service in 1961 from Finchley garage to replace trolleybuses and proved successful. These were initially classified ER (Extended Routemaster) but continued the Routemaster number sequence.

From 1965 all Routemaster buses were built new at 30ft long, gaining the classification RML, including the earlier ERs. These buses remained in active service until the end of Routemasters in normal service in 2005. They had 11.3-litre engines, rather than the standard 9.6-litre unit, due to their extra weight. There were also some 30ft Green Line coach Routemasters delivered in 1965, classified RCL. Again, all these variations maintained a consecutive number sequence.

RML2760 kept its original AEC engine throughout its life and was withdrawn from normal service in 2006, having been transferred to Stagecoach East London's special purposes fleet.

Although based at the London Bus Museum, RML2760 remains in Stagecoach ownership and is on long-term loan to the Museum.

The picture on the left shows preserved RML2760 outside the London Bus Museum at Brooklands.

RML2760 was approaching Trafalgar Square from the Strand in the main picture, heading towards Ladbroke Grove on the 15 route. The two yellow bands and yellow on the blinds were introduced in May 1985 to highlight the 15 as a tourist route, since it served the West End, City and Tower of London. It was a short-lived experiment.

DMS1

Following the trials with front-entrance, rear-engined double-deckers – 50 Park Royal bodied Leyland Atlanteans and 8 similar Daimler Fleetlines were bought in 1965 – and the experience gained with the troublesome AEC Merlin and Swift single-deckers, London Transport ordered a large number of two-door Daimler Fleetline double-deck buses. The first was delivered in late 1970. Hoping to continue the naming of bus types following the Routemaster, the new vehicle was designated The Londoner, but this did not catch on, perhaps because it looked to the general public no different from buses by now in use all over the country.

The DMS was the catalyst for the eventual abandonment of London Transport's famous overhaul procedures which, certainly for the RT family and the Routemaster, involved separating chassis and body. A trial overhaul of DMS1 resulted in body distortion.

By 1979 some 2,646 Fleetlines had been taken into stock, but continuing reliability issues had already resulted in earlier examples being withdrawn and sold. They were eagerly snapped up by other operators all over the UK and proved that, although the design was deemed *"not designed here and therefore not fit for London,"* they proved a godsend to most second users, who made them work quite efficiently.

DMS1 was shown new at the Commercial Motor Show in 1970 and then worked at a number of garages before withdrawal to store in 1982. It was placed with the London Transport Museum.

Route 220, on which these black and white photographs were taken, began on 20 July 1960 as a replacement for the long 630 trolleybus route which had run between Harrow Road/Scrubs Lane and West Croydon. The 220 was initially run with Routemasters, but became one of the first routes to use the DMS type at the beginning of 1971.

DMS1 was photographed in Hammersmith on 10 September 1971 in the picture on the opposite page.

Although the bus station here was named Butterwick, the name of the road in which it is alongside, few ever referred to it by that name.

Above, DMS1 was on layover in Longley Road, close to Tooting Station on 14 February 1971.

On the left, DMS1 was at the London Bus Museum TransportFest on 18 October 2015.

SMS369

Increasing staff shortages, particularly of conductors, and worsening traffic congestion had both been of growing concern to London Transport before its Reshaping Plan was published in 1966. This plan envisaged sweeping changes to the way that buses were to be operated, particularly in the suburbs. It envisaged wholesale adoption of one-person-operation, flat fares, single-deck buses to improve boarding and alighting times, and the shortening of routes to combat congestion and improve reliability.

With the plan adopted, it was necessary to embark on a large-scale programme of procurement of single-deckers to be built in both single- and dual-door format, equipped with automatic fare collection machinery and, in many cases, with a large 'standee' area to increase capacity on short routes.

Following initial trials in 1966 on Red Arrow routes designed to move commuters over short distances within central London, the plan was implemented from 1968 with the arrival of long AEC Merlins and shorter AEC Swifts in differing configurations.

There was widespread objection from the road staff unions over many issues connected both with the plan and with the buses themselves, which delayed their entry into service in several cases. Eventually, over 1,500 such buses were bought by London Transport, some of which were delivered in green livery for the Country Bus area.

Turning from Elstree Road onto High Road in Bushey Heath in the picture at the top of the opposite page, SMS369 was on a short-working of the 142.

SMS369 was operated by Edgware garage between February 1978 and January 1981.

Below, SMS369 was photographed in the London Bus Museum.

The Merlins and Swifts were beset almost from day one with mechanical reliability issues. These, and the fact that the design did not sit well with London Transport's then 'body-off' overhaul procedure, spelt their death knell and hundreds were withdrawn well before the end of their design life. Many were sold abroad, particularly to Malta, and some went to Northern Ireland to replace buses lost in the Troubles. Most went for scrap and few survived. SMS369 was withdrawn in 1980, having been one of the last five examples of its type still operating, and was sold for further service. Having passed through three owners, it was donated to the London Bus Museum in 1999.

Swift or Merlin

The Swift was AEC's offering for the rear-engined single-deck bus market. This chassis first appeared in 1964 after the takeover of AEC by Leyland and, in effect, was little more than a Leyland Panther with AEC mechanical units. The Swift was available in both 33ft and 36ft lengths.

AEC had also intended to market a heavy-duty Swift, for which it was going to use the name Merlin, but this heavy-duty chassis never materialised.

London Transport's first Swifts were 36ft long, like MBS420 on the right, photographed near East Grinstead Station in London Country colours in 1977, but were always referred to as Merlins rather than Swifts. However, when London Transport bought the shorter 33ft version, the Swift name was used.

RP 90

In 1965 London Transport bought a number of experimental buses to help shape its future buying policy. Included were 14 36ft single-deck AEC Reliances (designated RC) with air suspension and Willowbrook 'BET-style' long-windowed, dual-purpose bodies. Their 49 high-backed coach seats were intended to bring new levels of comfort to the Green Line network. They also sported a new Green Line livery of light grey with a broad green band, and were first put to work on the 705 between Windsor and Sevenoaks via Central London, Bromley and Westerham.

Public opinion was sought, as shown by the poster on the right, but they proved troublesome in service.

When London Transport's Country Area was passed over to the National Bus Company in 1970, forming London Country Bus Services, the new company inherited the RCs and bought similar AEC Reliances but with bodies built by Park Royal with many styling differences. They also reverted to a more traditional livery of Lincoln green with a pale green band.

There is evidence to suggest this plan was well advanced before the split, and the 90 RP-class one-person operated coaches were delivered in 1972. This enabled Green Line Routemaster coaches to be downgraded to bus work and ended the need for conductors on Green Line services.

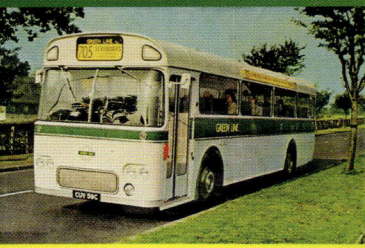

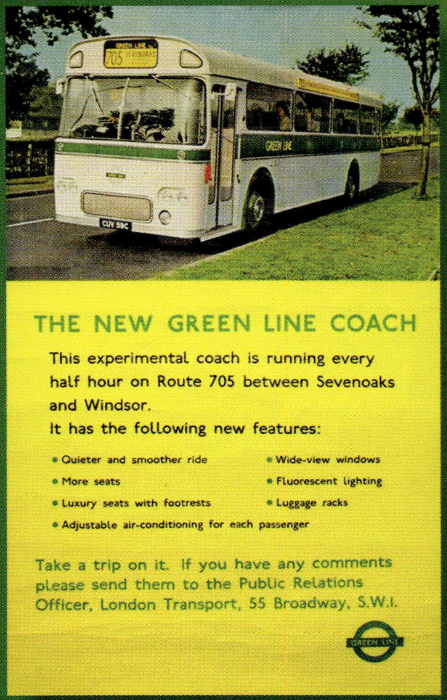
THE NEW GREEN LINE COACH
This experimental coach is running every half hour on Route 705 between Sevenoaks and Windsor.
It has the following new features:
• Quieter and smoother ride
• Wide-view windows
• More seats
• Fluorescent lighting
• Luxury seats with footrests
• Luggage racks
• Adjustable air-conditioning for each passenger
Take a trip on it. If you have any comments please send them to the Public Relations Officer, London Transport, 55 Broadway, S.W.1.
GREEN LINE

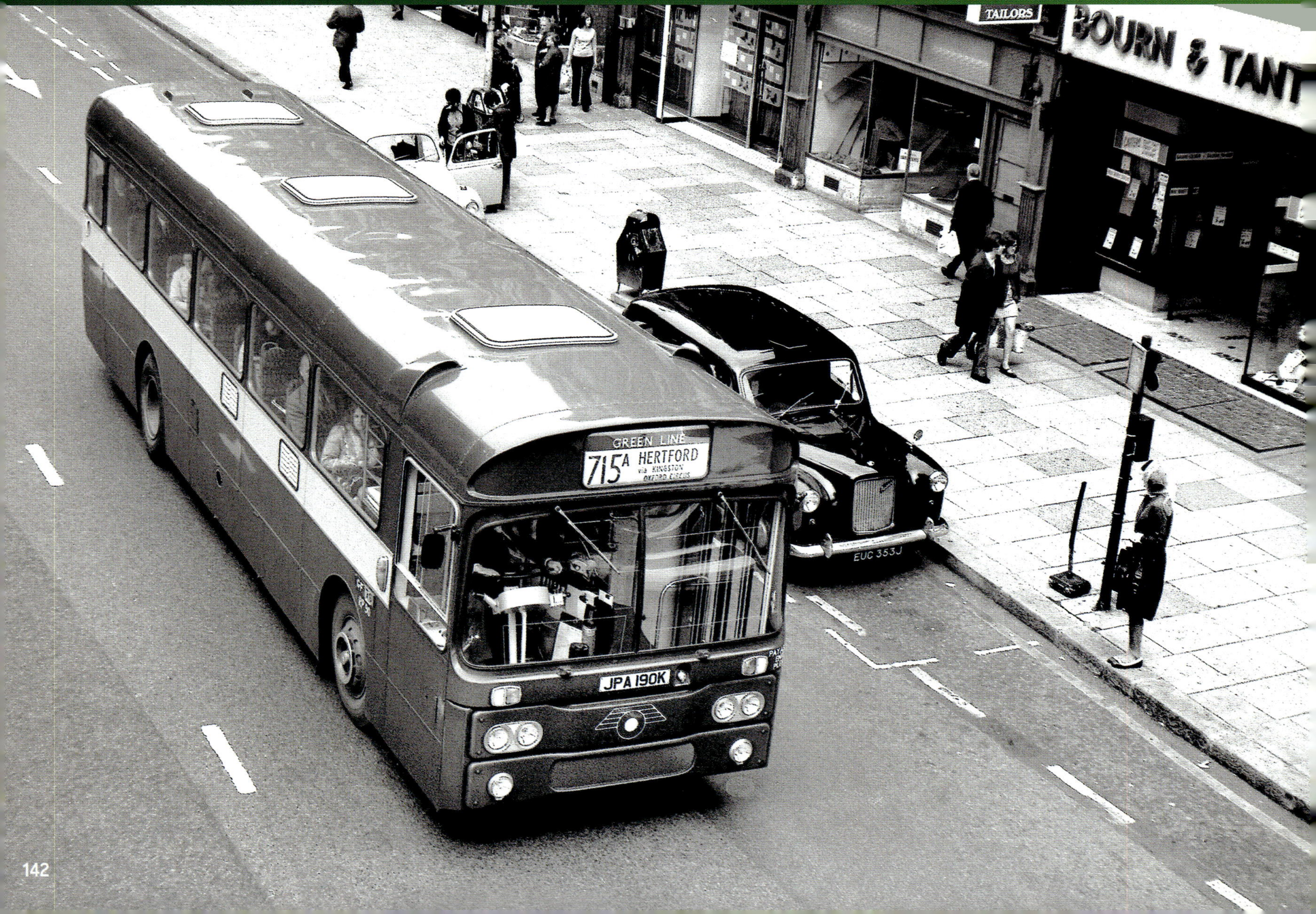
TAILORS
BOURN & TANT
GREEN LINE
715A HERTFORD
JPA 190K
EUC 353J

The picture on the opposite page
shows RP90 travelling along the north side of
Shepherd's Bush Green on 10 June 1972, when only two months old.

The windscreen and lower front panels were identical to those on London Country's contemporary Park Royal bodied Leyland Atlantean double-deck buses, which was probably intended to reduce the number of spare screens and panels needed in garage stores.

RP90 was working a London Bus Museum Open Day shuttle in the picture above, while below right, alongside preserved RCL2223, it was between duties at a Beer & Buses event on the Isle of Wight at Newport on 14 October 2018.

Towards the end of the days with London Country, the livery on the RPs lost its pale green waistline band when the vehicles succumbed to National Bus Company corporate livery, in this case a variation of the 'local coach' leaf green and white scheme. In this livery, RP90 was photographed in Hertford Bus Station on the cross-London Green Line 715A route to Guildford via Kingston.

M6

On this page are views of M6 in its original livery with white roundels and white upper deck window surrounds.

Metrobuses replaced DMS double-deckers on the West London route 90B from Kew Gardens Station via Richmond, Twickenham, Feltham and Hayes to Northolt Station in April 1979.

On the right, M6 was heading towards Northolt on a 90B working.

M6 was the first production Metrobus for London Transport and was delivered new to Fulwell. In the picture below it was in Teddington, heading to Fulwell garage on route 270 on 17 March 1979.

Fulwell Garage has a long history, having been opened as a tram depot by London United Tramways in 1902. Tracks still exist in the extensive yard. From 1931 until 1962, the depot operated a considerable number of trolleybuses, including examples of London's very first and very last classes.

With rear-engined double-deck buses predominating, the search was on for a replacement for the unsatisfactory DMS class. Leyland had produced the Titan with the London market very much in mind, but this would not meet the large requirement, initially or in total.

A stop-gap order for 164 Metro-Scania Metropolitans had impressed London Transport and consideration was given to adopting its successor, the Metrobus. This was in production by MCW at its Birmingham factory and, following trials with a demonstration vehicle, an order was placed for five buses to try out.

The trials were successful and orders were progressively placed, beginning in 1978. Eventually, nearly 1,500 Metrobuses, including second-hand examples, entered service in London throughout the network but, for engineering efficiency, tended to be allocated to specific garages.

After the tendering process for routes gathered momentum from 1986, many new and second-hand Metrobuses were added to the fleets of commercial operators winning those tenders. For example, Ensignbus, Capital Citybus, Blue Triangle, Connex and Grey-Green all bought Metrobuses.

On privatisation, M6 passed to the South London company at Croydon before becoming a training vehicle at Leaside Buses. Leaside became part of Arriva, and the bus was used to publicise Arriva's London version of its new corporate identity. It was bought for preservation in 2001 and was acquired by the London Bus Museum in 2003. Its original Automatic Fare Collection has been reinstated.

In preparation for the separate London Buses companies being set up in readiness for selling off, the bus livery was changed to this style on the left.

M6 was on the long Central London to Purley route 109 which had replaced trams in 1951. The skirt panels were a bit battered and the brightwork trim was missing from around the offside headlight here.

Below is M6 after acquisition by the London Bus Museum.

East London's T23 was heading south along Chapel Lane in Ilford in 1991 in the picture below, followed by T625.

In the picture on the right, T23 was in the London Bus Museum awaiting transfer on loan to the Bromley Bus Preservation Group, who have a collection of modern buses.

At the same time as the Metrobuses were joining the fleet, London Transport was also taking deliveries of Leyland's Titan, which had been designed largely with London requirements in mind. The first 250 buses were built by Park Royal Vehicles in West London, but the long-term viability of this plant was in doubt and all further examples were built at the Lillyhall factory in Workington in Cumbria, where the Leyland National single-deckers were being built, and which had spare capacity.

1,125 Titans in total were built for London between 1979 and 1984, with a further five acquired second-hand from West Midlands Passenger Transport Executive.

London Transport was finding it difficult to retain staff following deregulation of the bus operating sector outside London in 1986. Deregulation also led to the introduction of many more small single-deck buses, and a consequent surplus of big buses meant that the Titans began to be sold off. Former London Titans were bought in quantity by provincial operators and by those winning tenders from London Buses.

T23 was delivered in March 1979 and underwent just one overhaul at Aldenham works. It passed to Stagecoach East London in 1994, being operated from Romford's North Street garage, and was sold out of service to dealer Ensign in Essex in 2001. It then passed through four other owners before being acquired by the London Bus Museum in 2011.

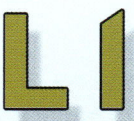

L1

Comparison trials were carried out on route 170 using the Leyland Olympian, Dennis Dominator and Metrobus in 1984.

In this picture, L1 was heading northwards through Roehampton, about to turn to its left to the terminus in Danebury Avenue.

In the background, rising up 230 feet, is the elegant spire of the late Victorian Holy Trinity church, built of fine Corsham stone.

The Olympian was Leyland's mainstay double-deck design that started full production in 1981 and continued as the Volvo Olympian after Volvo acquired Leyland Bus in 1988. It was, in effect, a version of the Leyland Titan integral double-decker, but with a separate chassis to hold the body, rather than the mechanical units being mounted within the body structure. To begin with, the Olympian was built at the former Bristol factory in Brislington, and the first thousand were completed here. But in 1983 production was transferred to Leyland's Farington and Workington plants.

In 1984 comparison trials were undertaken by London Buses under its Advanced Vehicle Engineering project on route 170, using three Leyland Olympians, three Dennis Dominators and two Mark II Metrobuses. Of the three, the Olympian was chosen and 260 were delivered in 1986 and 1987. They were bodied by Eastern Coach Works at Lowestoft. Ten had coach-style seats for use on special duties, including the X68 and 177 express routes, and thought to be more appealing for hiring out, too.

Further examples were later delivered for the standalone tendered operations, like Riverbus and Bexleybus, bodied by Leyland and Alexander respectively.

The first of the London Olympians, L1, was used initially as a trainer for garage engineers and then went to Croydon for ordinary service use. In due course it was acquired by Sussex bus operator Southern Transit for its heritage fleet.

L1 was at the East Anglia
Transport Museum at Carlton Colville
in July 2017 in the picture above. This was a special event at the
museum to commemorate the closure of Eastern Coach Works'
bodybuilding factory in Lowestoft 30 years earlier.

Below, L1 was at the delightful terminus of
Chipstead Valley in 1990.

OV2

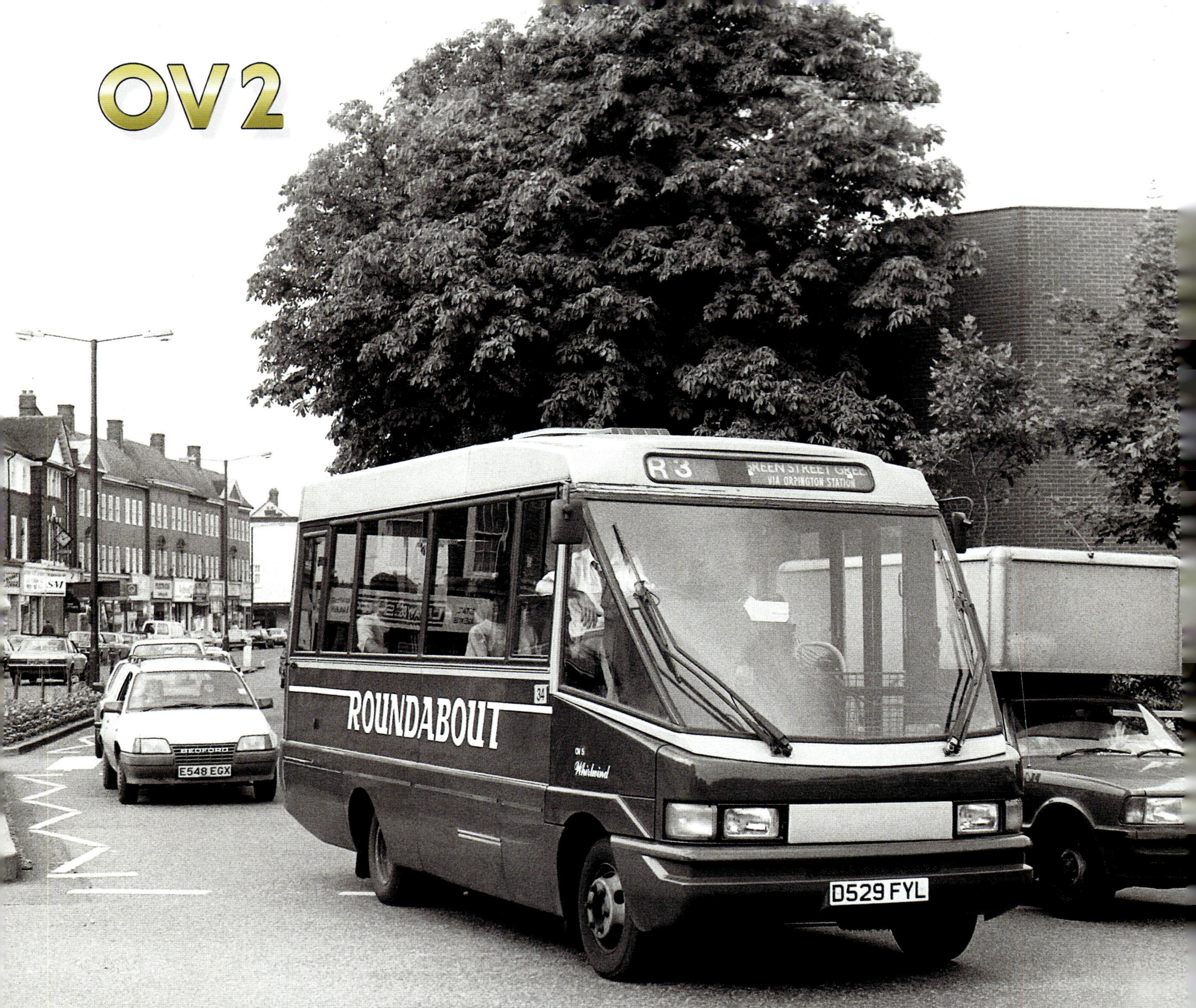

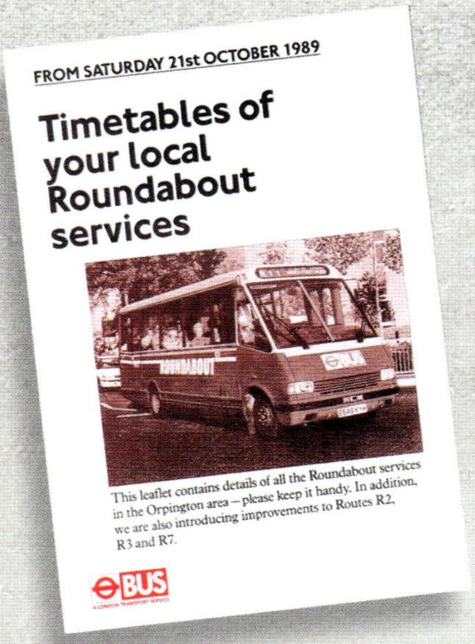
FROM SATURDAY 21st OCTOBER 1989

Timetables of your local Roundabout services

This leaflet contains details of all the Roundabout services in the Orpington area – please keep it handy. In addition, we are also introducing improvements to Routes R2, R3 and R7.

BUS

No in-service shot of OV2 has been found but, in the picture above, an identical OV5 was in Orpington High Street on 14 July 1989.

On the right, preserved OV2 was at Petts Wood Station on 13 August 2016 after having been on display earlier at an open day at Bromley garage.

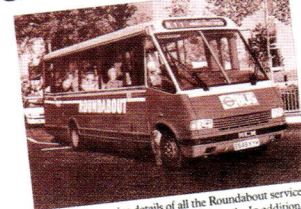

The introduction of the London Regional Transport Act in 1984 placed an obligation on the organisation to secure bus services under the most favourable terms. London Buses itself was broken up into smaller area units and tenders invited from commercial operators, too. The sale of those bus units in 1994/5 brought in names to the London market which had become familiar elsewhere in the UK, including Stagecoach and Go-Ahead. Given a little more autonomy within their own regimes, the new commercial operators began to introduce more innovative ways of supplying attractive local bus transport.

Manufacturers were already offering small buses which could penetrate residential areas more effectively and at lower cost, and they'd usually be run at higher frequencies. Volkswagen, Mercedes-Benz, Freight Rover, Renault-Dodge, Iveco, MCW and Dennis all had suitable products available. Most initial designs were based on pre-existing van bodies, including the Ford Transit, that weren't completely ideal. Inevitably, they attracted the derogatory term 'bread vans', because clearly that's what they were, albeit with side windows.

Optare offered the more stylish City Pacer based on Volkswagen van parts and produced five for the Roundabout network based in Orpington, where they operated alongside Iveco midibuses. Members of both types were given names and OV2, which is now in the London Transport Museum collection, is named Hurricane.

Optare supplied a further 47 City Pacers to various London bus operating units, including the central London minibus high-frequency network based at Victoria garage, Carelink, whose buses were equipped with wheelchair lifts and linked London's main railway terminals, and London Country North West, which had successfully tendered for the C2 route between Regent Street and Camden Town.

115

Leyland Bus, part of the British Leyland Group, went through hard times in the 1980s. This was partly because of the influx of, arguably, better quality products coming into the UK from foreign manufacturers. Leyland Bus went through a management buyout in 1987, but only a year later that management sold it to the Swedish builder, Volvo Bus Corporation.

Although some Leyland products, such as the Olympian bus chassis, were continued under Volvo ownership, increasingly Volvo's own designs began to predominate. Volvo was particularly strong in the single-deck and coach market with its underfloor-engined B10M chassis. This was also beginning to be used for double-deck buses but had the disadvantage of a high floor.

Long-established operator Grey-Green Coaches of Stamford Hill in North London had been owned by the Ewer Group, and this was taken over by the Cowie Group in 1980, as it decided to diversify from car sales and contract hire. With London bus routes being put out to tender, Cowie took the opportunity to move into London bus operation, using the Grey-Green name, still a well-known and respected transport brand.

High profile route 24 (Hampstead Heath - Pimlico) was the first bus route through the very centre of the capital to be put out to tender and was awarded to Grey-Green, which began running the route in November 1988. This was a coup for the company and allowed it to place brand-new double-deckers in a new Best Impressions designed version of Grey-Green's distinctive livery on a route which passed such landmarks as Trafalgar Square and the Houses of Parliament.

Heading for Brighton and in the Best Impressions designed livery, 115 had paused for a break at Pease Pottage Services on 6 May 2018 in the picture on the left.

The crew was comprised of London Transport Museum volunteers.

On the right, in service in all-over red livery in 1998, 115 was in Oakleigh Road in Whetstone.

The buses Grey-Green opted for were Volvo Citibus B10Ms with dual-door bodywork by Scottish builder Alexander of Falkirk. The initial 30 were followed by more, as other tendered routes were won, until the fleet eventually had 55.

Through a rather convoluted process of acquisitions and mergers, Cowie's bus operations metamorphosed into what became Arriva, a company that expanded into further bus and railway services across Europe and was later acquired by Deutsche Bahn.

Grey-Green 115 was part of the first B10M fleet for the 24. It was subsequently repainted to conform with TfL's newly-introduced requirement that buses on tendered routes had to be red. 115 was withdrawn in 2003. As a preserved bus, it was repainted into its original Grey-Green colours and placed on loan to the London Transport Museum.

Another famous London coach company in the Ewer Group was Orange Luxury Coaches of Brixton in South London, which had this impressive coach station facing Effra Road built in 1927. At one time there was a large banner under the arch announcing trips daily to "all seaside resorts".

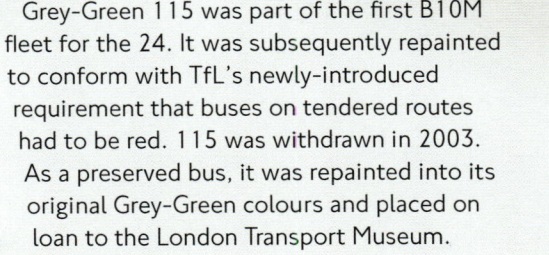

In the main picture, MA1 was leaving Bakers Road Bus Station in Uxbridge on 18 May 1992, working for CentreWest on local route U2 to Hillingdon Hospital.

Below on the right is a view looking down on MA1 in the London Transport Museum. By now the midibus was carrying its Uxbridge Buses identity.

Among the myriad numbers of mini- and midi-buses put into service by London bus operators were the Mercedes and Dennis Darts purchased by CentreWest Buses.

Routes 28 (Wandsworth - Golders Green) and 31 (Chelsea - Camden Town) traversed a complex network of roads across parts of West London using Routemasters, but these routes were becoming notorious for buses getting caught up in traffic congestion. So, controversially at the time, they were converted to midibus operation in 1988, primarily at the instigation of Peter Hendy (later Commissioner of Transport for London, and now Lord Hendy of Richmond Hill, of Imber in the County of Wiltshire) under the trading name Gold Arrow.

The buses could get very crowded in service, but nonetheless patronage increased by 70%.

Other local networks also were given Mercedes midibuses, including what became U-Line services in the Uxbridge area, and services from Putney and Victoria, branded Streetline. There were also five midibuses with wheelchair lifts for Mobility Bus operations.

Mercedes MA1 was kept by FirstGroup after withdrawal from service and is now preserved in conjunction with the London Transport Museum.

DW15

Dennis Brothers was founded in Guildford in 1895 and throughout its existence encompassed nearly every type of motor vehicle and, although particularly associated with fire appliances and municipal vehicles, it did build buses and coaches too.

After the deregulation of the bus operating industry, Dennis quickly recognised that the small-bus revolution demanded a purpose-built product, rather than the converted van-type solution. In 1990 Dennis released the Dart. This was at first an 8.5m long chassis, initially bodied in a distinctive and unusual style by Duple, itself a long-established name in the bus and coach industry. Wright's of Ballymena in Northern Ireland offered a more traditional but rather utilitarian-looking design in the Handybus. The Dart was bought in hundreds by London operators and many others across the UK, bodied by most of the commercial bus builders.

DW15 was new to CentreWest, one of the London Buses companies, for the Gold Arrow services from Westbourne Park garage in 1991. CentreWest was sold to its management in 1994. The bus has a Northern Irish registration number, because the batch, along with several others, was registered new by Wright's, rather than by the London operator.

CentreWest was sold on to FirstGroup in 1997, and DW15 later transferred within First to First Beeline at Bracknell and then to First Cymru in Swansea. It was retrieved for the London Transport Museum in 2005 and refurbished by Wright's into original Gold Arrow livery.

DW midibuses were introduced on the 105 route in March 1995. On 5 April 1996 DW15 was photographed at Southall in the picture on the left. The Challenger fleetname was the local identity used for a time by FirstGroup for services from its Alperton garage.

Above, just over 20 years later, it was on the route 31 Running Day on 8 October 2017 and, on the right, being prepared for the event by London Transport Museum volunteers.

The increasing desire, demand and need for fewer (in fact, zero) impediments to boarding a bus by anyone, but especially by those with mobility restrictions, using wheelchairs or pushing child buggies, led to the development of what became known as the low-floor bus. These were designed with level boarding and no steps for most of the length of the lower deck gangway, plus a dedicated space for a wheelchair user to position themselves securely for the journey. Kneeling suspension, activated by releasing air, was incorporated to reduce the boarding height still further.

The Public Service Vehicle Accessibility Regulations 2000 (PSVAR), applied to all buses of more than 22 seats operating on local or scheduled services, came into force for all new buses and coaches from the very beginning of 2001.

London General's WVL1 is a Volvo-powered Wrightbus Gemini, which entered service from Stockwell Garage in March 2002. There have been many Wright Gemini bodied buses introduced to several London bus fleets, together with similar low-floor models from the UK's other main bus builder, Alexander Dennis.

WVL1 was withdrawn in 2017, having given a very creditable 15 years' service battling London's traffic. Through the kindness of bus dealer Ensignbus, the London Bus Museum has been able to show the continually evolving state of London bus design.

On the opposite page, WVL1 was photographed in Peckham on 24 June 2002.

The London Bus Museum organised a successful route 93 running day in 2021 and in the picture above, WVL1 was in Dorking opposite the White Hart.

EB2

Huge strides have been made across the global automotive industry to find the least polluting and most economic motor vehicles. This revolution was also embraced by bus and coach operators, and manufacturers were soon to offer a wide variety of motive power sources, including external-feed electricity, battery, hydrogen fuel cell and hybrid. Transport for London has been a keen advocate of green transportation and by early 2022 London Buses had already converted over 50% of its fleet to hybrid and pure electric power, with the intention for the entire fleet to be zero-emission by 2030.

The Chinese manufacturer BYD produced two pioneering all-electric buses for trial in London in 2013, EB1 and EB2. They operated on Red Arrow routes 507 and 521. BYD kindly placed EB2 on long-term loan to the London Bus Museum in 2021. Its lithium-iron phosphate battery gives approximately 150 miles of urban operation on a single charge. This vehicle was put on display with the electrical equipment cabinets fronted in clear Perspex for visitors to see how these are accommodated within the bus.

Here is EB2 at Victoria Station on a short working of the former 507 Red Arrow route between Victoria and Waterloo via Lambeth Bridge.

what next?

Time moves on, today becomes history and no museum can stand still, unless it has deliberately set a closed time period. The history of London buses moves ever onward and vehicles which are in service today will themselves become candidates for preservation. Who knows what future preservationists will choose? Three possibilities are illustrated here.

The Wrightbus New Bus for London was the result of then Mayor, Boris Johnson's nostalgic desire for a modern Routemaster to have a conductor and allow boarding and alighting between bus stops.

It has three sets of doors, the rearmost wrapping round a rear platform which could be open or closed. There was also initially what was called a passenger services attendant (once known as a conductor).

Power is hybrid electric, with a small diesel engine mounted under the rear stairs. The bodywork styling was by the Heatherwick Studio and all 1,000 buses were built in Northern Ireland. LT85 in the picture above was new for London United in 2013.

Mercedes-Benz Citaro articulated bendybuses were first introduced to London in 2001, but all had gone by 2011. The upper picture on the right shows London General MAL117.

Abellio London's 3436 on the right was built by BYD with an Alexander-Dennis Enviro 400 City body. It is an electric zero-emission bus powered by batteries.

Today's technology could prove to be a challenge for future preservationists!

We are extremely grateful to everyone who has allowed us to use their photographs to help tell the story, and we have done everything we can to show them off to their best advantage.

On the right is a list of the photographers and the pages on which you can find their photos.

We also thank the following people for their invaluable contributions to this project:

Peter, Lord Hendy of Richmond Hill
Leon Daniels OBE
Sam Mullins OBE
for their forewords

Laurie Akehurst
for guidance on the detail of Rover tickets

Graham Smith
David Bowker
Peter Larkham
John Hewitt
for proofreading.

And, lastly, we must pay tribute to all the many previous researchers and authors, whose articles and books have been consulted.

Tony Belton
85 upper

David Bowker
31 upper

The Bus Archive
30
50 lower
59 upper

J S Cockshott
106

Alan B Cross
36
37 lower/middle
38 lower
39
40
43
45
46
47 lower
49 upper
50 lower
52 upper
53 upper/middle
58
63
65 upper
65 lower right
67 upper
68
71 upper/lower
72 lower
74
79 lower
80 upper
81
82 lower
87
91 lower
92
94
97 lower
98
101
103 upper
105 upper
108
114 lower
120
122 lower
125
135 upper
138
139 upper
141 upper

Damon Cross
114 upper
145 lower
147
157 upper

Leon Daniels
16 upper
42
52 lower
62
80 lower
96 upper
104 lower
128
130 upper
136
140
143 upper
155

Michael Dryhurst
85 lower
99 upper

Nigel Eadon-Clarke
50 upper

Russell Fell / The Transport Library
146
150
154

Colin Fradd
137
143 lower left

Andy Gray
149 lower

Tom Gurney
151

Roger Hall
160

Mike Harris
130 lower
144 upper
145 upper

Jim Hawkins
11 lower

Fred Ivey
7
11 upper
49 lower
54 upper
55
56
75
84
121 lower
122 lower

Nigel Lemon
32 lower

London Transport Museum
14
15
17 upper
19 upper
23
29
35 lower
116 upper
117 left

Guy Marriott
10
31 lower
35 upper
113 left

Glyn Matthews
95 lower left

Ian Read
20
44 lower
54 lower
82 upper
96 lower
143 lower right
157 lower

Roger Stagg
116 lower left

Colin Stannard
5
129
131 upper
142
144 lower
148
153 upper
156
158

Ray Stenning
8
9
66
89
97 upper
103 lower
104 upper
109 lower
110
112
118
122 upper
123 lower
126
127
132
133
134 lower
135 lower
141 lower
159

John Stiles
17 lower
18 upper
19 lower
21 upper
22
25
26
27 lower
28
32 upper right
33 upper
37 upper
38 upper
47 upper
48
51
64
65 lower left
70
71 middle
78
79 upper
83
86
91 upper
93
95
99 lower
100
102
107 upper right
121 upper
123 upper
124
134 upper
139 lower

Denis Strange
3 lower

Terry Torch
161 lower

Richard Wallace
152

Watford Libraries
24

Barry Weatherhead Collection
33 lower

Jim Whiting
88
115

Peter Zabek
4
34
41 upper
59 lower
61
69
72 upper
73
90
105 lower

While every effort has been made at accurate attributions, we apologise for any errors or omissions which may have crept in.